PRACTICAL

TAEKWONDO

Back to the Roots
Matthew Sylvester

summersdale

Summersdale Publishers Ltd
46 West Street
Chichester
West Sussex
PO19 1RP
UK

www.summersdale.com

Published in association with Matthew Sylvester

Typeset in Gillsans 11pt by
Chandler Book Design, King's Lynn, Norfolk
www.chandlerbookdesign.co.uk

Printed and bound by
the MPG Books Group in the UK

ISBN: 978-1-84024-758-9

Substantial discounts on bulk quantities of Summersdale books are available to corporations, professional associations and other organisations. For details telephone Summersdale Publishers on (+44-1243-771107), fax (+44-1243-786300) or email (nicky@summersdale.com).

DEDICATIONS

Without my wife Karen being there, not only as a test dummy in the early days of Practical Taekwondo™, but also as a staunch, loyal and loving supporter, I'd never have been able to get off my arse and write this book. I love you babes.

Without Rick Clark and Ken and Jayne Tucker my eyes would never have been opened (nor closed so often) as to the possibilities of pressure points, nor how to find them in the martial art I could never get away from. I'd like to thank Jayne for letting me stay over so often and bore her silly with martial arts waffle.

Without Bill Burgar I'd never had had such a good rating system to use.

Without Geoff Thompson's *Shapeshifter*, and having spoken to him, I would have never realised that I could change the way I am in a positive manner.

Without Iain Abernethy I'd never have the *Mental Strength* to do this sort of thing (good plug, Google it). So it's his fault, not mine.

Without Pres. Choi Jung Hwa I would never have been so inspired as to truly believe in myself and the good that Taekwondo can do in the world.

Without Jim Wagner and Lee Sansum I'd never have been able to experience being a bodyguard 'for real', nor would I be as hard a target as I am.

Without Ray being such a willing test dummy and Phil and Zak photographers, this would have been impossible to do.

Finally thanks to my family for always being there to help us out, it hasn't been easy. Mum, Ann, and Fi, your help is always appreciated and never taken for granted.

Ragan and Kira, you're my little angels. Your constant interruptions for hugs and help are something that most daddies don't get when they're at work. I'm a very lucky daddy to have you two.

Enjoy the book.

CONTENTS

Foreword

FOREWORD

LAWRENCE KANE

A common complaint I've heard time and again is that taekwondo is merely a sport, simply not practical for defending oneself on the street where adversaries are not constrained by tournament rules and civil niceties. Heck, I've experienced examples of this phenomenon myself, such as when an unruly football fan tried to whack me upside the head with a Bandae Dollyo Chagi (Spinning Roundhouse/Reverse Turning Kick) at a stadium where I was working security. A green belt in karate at the time, I nevertheless easily shifted inside his range, scoop-blocked his technique, captured his leg, and dragged him over to a waiting police officer. During the arrest I discovered that my assailant was a black belt in taekwondo. Why was I able to defeat a vastly more skilled attacker? Because I stuck to straightforward, mechanically sound movements that took less time to execute than my attacker's impractical technique.

And that, my friends, is where Matthew Sylvester's outstanding book comes into play. It is jam-packed with terrific advice, the kind of stuff that has been sorely needed in the taekwondo community for a very long time. Perusing it you will quickly discover that as *kata* forms the heart of traditional karate, patterns form the core of practical taekwondo. The challenge is that most practitioners see these patterns as a waste of time; they neither know what they mean nor how to use them effectively. If your goal is to win an Olympic medal or compete effectively in a sparring ring then you probably shouldn't care all that much about the true breadth and depth of *patterns*, but if you want the ability to defend yourself successfully on the street you'd best pay close attention.

With excellent writing and clear illustrations, Sylvester demonstrates how to perform a variety of street-worthy self-defence applications from the Saju Jirugi, Chon Ji, and Taegeuk Il Jang patterns, pressure test them, and tailor the techniques to fit your personal predilections and body type. Once you discover how technique-rich these three simple patterns can be, you can easily apply what you have learned to the rest of your patterns as well. You will quickly realise that taekwondo can, and should, be far more than mere kicking and punching. For example, what you have always thought of as 'blocks' are defensive in nature, yet they act more like strikes in practical application. The patterns also demonstrate throws, locks, takedowns, chokes, pressure point applications, and a whole lot more.

So, who is this Sylvester guy, and why should you listen to him anyway? To begin with, he is a Reality Based Personal Protection Instructor (Black Belt Hall of Fame member Jim Wagner's system) who has earned black belts in Jung Shin Taekwondo, Ao Denkou Jitsu, and Aikoushin Kobujitsu, and pressure tested his skills as a special constable and door supervisor. For years he has dedicated himself to making taekwondo as functional and street-worthy as possible, banding together with like-minded instructors throughout the UK and Ireland to develop Practical Taekwondo™ an organisation that looks to recover the oft-forgotten martial aspects of the art. His columns in *Combat*, *Traditional Karate*, and *Taekwondo & Korean Martial Arts* magazines are internationally renowned.

This outstanding book is well written and thoroughly illustrated. It shows a plethora of practical techniques, but also goes an important step farther by taking you through a process for uncovering your own street-worthy applications from patterns. The author demonstrates how to sensibly pressure test and judge the effectiveness of what you discover so that you can discover what works for you without risking grave bodily injury and a whole lot of pain in the process of finding out. Sylvester offers sound advice that all taekwondo practitioners should pay close attention to.

Lawrence Kane
Author of *Surviving Armed Assaults* and *Martial Arts Instruction*; co-author of *The Way of Kata* and *The Way to Black Belt*.

INTRODUCTION

Practical Taekwondo – Back to the roots is a series of books that acknowledges the fact that the Tuls/Hyungs are based on Japanese patterns, namely those of the Heian and Pinan family. Do not expect an in-depth history on this however as this is the not the purpose of the book.

It is clear that the Chang Hun Tuls are really just remixes of the original Japanese Heians, especially if you compare such patterns as Won Hyo and Heian Nidan. The up-thrust of this is that many of the applications/oyo found in the Japanese martial arts can easily be found within the Tul.

Similarly, the Palgwes and Taegeuk Poomsae are also linked (albeit with a larger degree of separation) to the Heian and Pinan forms. Indeed, the motion used for such blocks as the Low Block is remarkably similar to that of karate.

Practical Taekwondo – Back to the roots, will take taekwondo practitioners through a journey of discovery, opening the eyes of many practitioners to the fact that taekwondo has far more to offer than is currently realised. This book makes no claims that these are the only applications, the official applications or any other such claim. The applications within this book are ones that I have used and taught during my study of the art. They are illustrations as to what can be found, how it can be found and how it can be assessed. Some you will like and take as your own, others you might find are not to your liking. However, as an instructor it is all too easy to teach what works for *you*, without taking into consideration what works for *others*.

It is important that you find applications and techniques that you are happy with and which work for you personally. Also please bear in mind that all of the techniques presented here are being presented in a nice safe environment with a level floor, good lighting, and compliant partners. These are the 'ideal' techniques, that is, *if* everything went to plan this is what would happen. However, when you're in a situation which requires the use of techniques like these, or others that you have found, you may well find that you are not going to be able to perform them perfectly. This could be due to the fact that you have consumed alcohol, or that the ground under your feet is icy, slick, or uneven. However, a 'failed' wrist lock (which can rely on Fine Motor Skills) can still be used to gain a release rather than a lock. It is important that you continue your defence regardless as to whether any one technique works or 'fails'.

Nor should you regard (for example) a wrist lock attempt not working as a failure, as you will still be altering the mental state of your attacker from that of attacker to defender. This will give you an opening which you can exploit by resorting to Gross Motor techniques such as punching, biting and gouging (for example).

Not only is taekwondo a percussive martial art, it has takedowns, chokes, locks and throws and all of these can be found within the patterns that are taught the world over.

This is not a taekwondo theory book however. Whilst the stances, weapons and pressure points used in the various patterns will be detailed, this book should in no way be used to replace any theory books that you already have, rather it should compliment your library and improve your practical skills.

The purpose of this book is to show the reader how they can start discovering their own techniques and use the rating system to judge their effectiveness.

I hope that you enjoy reading this book as much as I have enjoyed writing it.

WHAT IS 'PRACTICAL TAEKWONDO™'?

Practical Taekwondo™ is both a label and a concept. As a label it sets what I do aside from the public perceptions of 'what taekwondo is'. Many readers will have noticed how I spell taekwondo. When I first started, it was with the Tae Kwon Do Association of Great Britain (TAGB) who spelt it Tae Kwon Do. General Choi spells it Taekwon-Do. Because I am not a member of the International Taekwon-Do Federation (ITF), I did not want to spell it in the General's way, in order to avoid confusion should ITF students come to me for training and expect ITF-like classes.

Many people have visions of taekwondo being similar to karate in that students wear doboks and march up and down Church Halls kicking, punching and shouting, and performing impressively high kicks.

Many other people have seen taekwondo in the Olympics and perceive it to be two people bouncing up and down on their toes.

The use of the label 'Practical Taekwondo' sets it aside from both and also implies that it can be 'used' practically.

The concept is somewhat more difficult to define. There are two ways of looking at this.

1. Practical Taekwondo™ is an attempt to return to the roots of taekwondo and study the martial aspects of the style (not art) that have been lost

due to various levels of ignorance (due to instructors not being shown the applications in the first place), deliberate choice, and the rise of the sporting aspect.

2. Practical Taekwondo™ is an eclectic art that takes elements of other arts and incorporates them into this style.

Practical Taekwondo™ is option one. It isn't sport. Is sparring done? Yes, but not for points or competition. Sparring is used because it helps apply the techniques and moves taught in class against a completely non-compliant partner. Sparring isn't done to 'win' but to learn. If someone gets a tapout it's not a 'win', merely an indicator as to how well they are progressing in their training.

There are various types of sparring:

*   using just hands

*   using just feet

*   using just feet and hands

*   using just grappling

*   using every tool in our arsenal

*   sparring to get specific techniques from within the patterns

*   sparring using the self-defence applications

*   There is no classic three or two step 'sparring'. The self-defence applications are based on one step attacks utilising for example, haymakers, Front Kicks, grabs to hand, shoulder and chest, from the front, side and back. All of the Habitual Acts of Violence (HAOV) that we think we will encounter in *our* area are covered, with the most likely attacks being devoted the most space.

Practical Taekwondo™ isn't meant to be, nor is it designed to be, an ultimate martial art or indeed a distinct martial art. It is one interpretation as to how taekwondo could or should be.

Nor does Practical Taekwondo™ rely on pressure points to solve the problem. Practical Taekwondo™ emphasises that a good and powerful delivery system is key to removing the attacker. However, because of the usefulness of pressure points they are utilised in every application.

Unlike other forms of taekwondo, Practical Taekwondo™ utilises the movements in the patterns to sweep, reap, and perform throws as part of the core syllabus, rather than as extra-curricular training. Every one of the techniques listed can be found in the patterns. It doesn't matter if they are taught or not, sweeps, buckles and throws are part and parcel of the patterns. As the patterns are the core of Practical Taekwondo™ then it can't be called eclectic, it can however be called 'classical' but that's a completely different subject.

Practical Taekwondo™ believes in training in a realistic manner, training is not practised in doboks but in dobok bottoms, t-shirts and trainers, as well as normal clothing. Scenarios using swearing and props are utilised so that students can become conditioned to the use of bad language and the sight of blood and not be mentally overwhelmed.

Practical Taekwondo™ lets our students know and appreciate what it feels like to be hit. This is both through the use of controlled contact in the self-defence applications, and in our sparring. It is important for the students to become conditioned to strikes in a relaxed and friendly atmosphere so that they are not surprised by the experience on the street.

Practical Taekwondo™ also take pains to emphasise that these techniques are ideals only, that is, they are training in a nice and warm environment with their friends and that each technique taught is being taught with the most optimistic outcome resulting. There is no guarantee when it comes to real fighting; however Practical Taekwondo™ does its utmost to prepare students for this.

Finally, Practical Taekwondo™ encourages students to look outside of the box and to train in other styles. Many of our students have come from other styles, and indeed are still training in those styles and we believe that their experiences and knowledge can only help us to grow both personally and as a concept. Currently in my class for example, I have students from ITF Taekwon-Do, the TAGB, Krav Maga, Ninjutsu and Wing Chun. All of these students have just as much to offer to us as we have to offer them.

Because Practical Taekwondo™ is a concept and not a style, it allows people from all forms of taekwondo who practice the Taegeuks, Chang Hon, Palgwe and Pyong-Ahn patterns to apply it to their style. Some will continue to teach competition taekwondo whilst using Practical Taekwondo™ concepts for self-defence classes; others will embrace the concept fully. Either approach is fine as one of the most important factors of the concepts is that taekwondo is *your* art.

Key factors of the concept:

- Patterns are the core of taekwondo.

- Self-defence applications should be drawn from the patterns, but advanced students may well draw applications that utilise techniques from more than one pattern.

- Self-defence applications should be pressure tested (applying the applications against a progressively resistant partner).

- Self-defence applications cannot be exclusive when taught to a class, that is, they have to work for everyone.

- Self-defence applications should be tailored and adapted so that they work for *you*. If they don't work, don't practice them.

- Sparring is a learning experience, cooperate and help others learn how to apply the techniques taught.

- Self-defence applications are ideals. As soon as you start sparring you will most likely find you can only apply sections of them, or even a string of sections. That is perfectly OK and to be expected.

- Self-defence applications are teaching tools, they show the students how to attack various targets, using the 'correct' tools.

- Pressure points are not magical. You don't need to hum, think of colours or worry about 'fire burns wood' theories. If you hit them they work on 80 per cent of the population. So concentrate on your core weapons and get good at hitting. Never rely on a pressure point to finish a fight for you, always have something to back it up.

- Only do enough to stop an attacker, never continue striking them once they have stopped attacking, or ceased to be a threat.

2

THE WEAPONS OF SAJU JIRUGI, CHON-JI AND TAEGEUK IL JANG

The three patterns[1] that this book covers are often considered to be simple and to contain basic movements. However, in my research over the last five years, I have found them to be technique-rich.

If you take the patterns at face value they contain the Low Block, the Inward Outer Fore Arm Block, the Outward Inner Forearm Block, the Rising Block and the punch. All of these are perfectly valid weapons in their own right and can be used to devastating effect as they are. It should not be assumed, however, that these are the only weapons available to you in these patterns.

It should be remembered that patterns *cannot* contain every application, for every technique. Patterns are merely shorthand guides that contain specific movements that are demonstrated as techniques. This does not mean that if you're too close to punch you aren't following the pattern if you Elbow. It does mean that you're following the movement of the pattern, and shaping the weapon for the target and situation. Do not become bound by the movements, but use them to point you in the right direction.

During the course of my research into these patterns and their applications I have found the following weapons. It should also be borne in mind that I consider blocks to be valid tools for striking attackers. For simplification, however, I will still call them blocks when using them to strike.

---

[1] Pedants: It is accepted that Saju Jirugi is not officially a pattern; however, this book shall treat it as so.

PUNCH

For taking the attacker's balance

Easily converted into a Palm Heel or Elbow depending on situation and range

For using as a Shoulder Strike

For pulling the attacker in (when chambering)

LOW BLOCK

Also very good for smashing with the forearm or wrist

Elbow (for those using the hip-twist chamber)

Simultaneous parry and counter-punch (for those using the World Taekwondo Federation [WTF] chamber)

Centre Lock

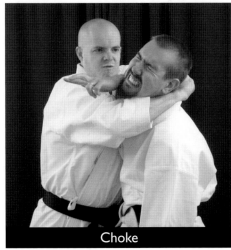

Choke

INWARD OUTER FOREARM BLOCK

Hammer Fist

Trapping/wrapping

RISING BLOCK

Also very good for Forearm Strikes to vulnerable points such as the neck

Also valid as an Uppercut

Also valid as a Shovel Hook

2 OUTWARD INNER FOREARM BLOCK

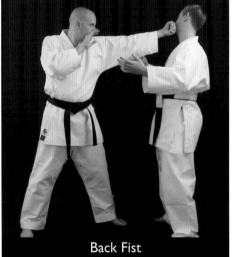

Back Fist

Thumb Fist

WALKING STANCE/ FRONT STANCE

2

Buckles

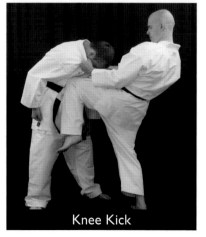

Knee Kick

Leg/knee attacks

FRONT SNAP KICK

Stamping attack

Jam against kicks

Outer reaping throw

Forward Stance

For weapons see above *Walking Stance*.

3

THE STANCES OF SAJU JIRUGI, CHON-JI AND TAEGEUK IL JANG

Stances are not often given the full respect they deserve. Performed correctly they can take an attacker to the ground, destroy their knees, attack their legs and increase the power of your strikes.

All of the patterns start with Chunbi-Stance, also known as Ready or Neutral Stance.

There are only four different stances used in Saju Jirugi, Chon-Ji and Taegeuk Il Jang.

- Saju Jirugi uses the ITF Walking Stance, which is known as the Front Stance in the WTF.

- Chon-Ji uses both the Walking Stance and the L-Stance.

- Taegeuk Il Jang uses the Front Stance (Walking Stance in ITF) and the WTF Walking Stance, which is much higher and shorter than the more traditional-looking Front Stance.

CHUNBI/READY STANCE

Chunbi stance from front

Chunbi stance from side

Every pattern starts with some version of Chunbi. At the end of the pattern, students return to Chunbi before moving on to their next pattern or next technique. It is used to signal that the student is ready to commence whatever exercise the instructor requires them to.

The feet should be roughly one shoulder width apart with the weight distribution being 50–50. The hands are usually held at belt height with the arms being slightly bent.

Moving into Chunbi is very easy. Usually it is the right foot that is drawn from whatever position it is in until you are facing the front of the dojang.

Student in right ITF Walking Stance, captured from the right side

Student draws their right foot backward whilst turning to the right (towards the camera)

Student finishes turning towards the camera and is in Chunbi

Walking Stance from front

Walking Stance from side

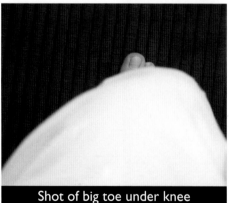

Shot of big toe under knee

In the Walking Stance/Front Stance, the weight distribution is equal. The lead leg should be bent far enough forward that only the tip of the big toe is visible over the knee. In both versions the stance is usually 1.5 shoulder widths deep and one shoulder width wide. The lead foot points directly forward and the rear foot points at a roughly 30° angle.

L-Stance from front

L-Stance from side

The L-Stance (Back Stance in WTF) is so-called because the feet create an 'L' shape on the floor. The weight distribution is different from the others with 70 per cent being placed on the back foot.

Because the majority of the weight is on the back foot, the stance is better suited towards defensive techniques and front-leg kicks.

The feet are roughly 1.5 shoulder widths apart with the heels of both feet aligned. The front foot points directly to the front and the rear foot points 90° sideways to the left or right. Both knees are bent with the rear knee being bent slightly more than the lead leg.

WTF WALKING STANCE

WTF Walking Stance from front

WTF Walking Stance from side

In the Walking Stance the weight distribution is equal between both feet. It is very mobile and is well-suited for launching kicks and punches equally. The feet are roughly one shoulder-width apart and the stance is roughly one shoulder-width deep.

The front foot points directly forward with the rear foot pointing outward at roughly 30°.

MOVING FORWARD IN THE WALKING STANCE (ITF)

The Walking Stance has long been underestimated. Although many view its width and depth as being unrealistic for the street this is because they have been looking at it as an absolute stance rather than a transitionary stance.

There are two ways that you can move forward. The first is the 'crescent' method and the second is the 'step' method.

Although the most common method to move forward is the crescent method, there is no reason that the stepping method cannot be used. It should be borne in mind however, that due to the low nature of the stance, the crescent is easier to perform. The crescent also allows the student to cock their hip should they be moving forward to punch. This, therefore, allows them to strike with greater impact upon landing.

CRESCENT METHOD

The rear foot describes an arc on the floor, moving in towards the lead foot

Halfway through the movement the feet are parallel to each other, some people touch them together at this point

The foot continues to describe the arc on the floor until it reaches the correct place at the front

3

THE STANCES OF SAJU JIRUGI, CHON-JI AND TAEGEUK IL JANG

STEPPING METHOD

The rear foot steps forward 90°

Halfway through the movement the feet are parallel to each other and one shoulder width apart

The foot continues forward until it reaches the correct place at the front

Rather than repeat a similar set of images representing how to move back, please refer to the above pictures in *reverse* order to understand the following instructions.

CRESCENT METHOD

1. The lead foot describes an arc on the floor, moving in towards the rear foot.

2. Halfway through the movement the feet are parallel to each other, some people touch them together at this point.

3. The foot continues to describe the arc on the floor until it reaches the correct place at the rear

STEPPING METHOD

1. The lead foot steps forward 90°.

2. Halfway through the movement the feet are parallel to each other and one shoulder width apart.

3. The foot continues forward until it reaches the correct place at the rear

3

THE STANCES OF SAJU JIRUGI, CHON-JI AND TAEGEUK IL JANG

MOVING FORWARD IN WALKING STANCE (WTF)

Although the most common method to move forward is the stepping method, there is no reason that the crescent method cannot be used. It should be borne in mind however that due to the high nature of the stance the step is easier to perform.

CRESCENT METHOD

The rear foot describes an arc on the floor, moving in towards the lead

Halfway through the movement the feet are parallel to each other, some people touch them together at this point

The foot continues to describe the arc on the floor until it reaches the correct place at the front

STEPPING METHOD

The rear foot steps forward 90°

Halfway through the movement the feet are parallel to each other and one shoulder width apart

The foot continues forward until it reaches the correct place at the front

MOVING BACKWARD IN
WALKING STANCE (WTF)

Rather than repeat a similar set of images representing how to move back, please refer to the above pictures in *reverse* order to understand the following instructions.

CRESCENT METHOD

1. The lead foot describes an arc on the floor, moving in towards the rear foot.

2. Halfway through the movement the feet are parallel to each other, some people touch them together at this point.

3. The foot continues to describe the arc on the floor until it reaches the correct place at the rear.

STEPPING METHOD

1. The lead foot steps forward 90°.

2. Halfway through the movement the feet are parallel to each other and one shoulder width apart.

3. The foot continues forward until it reaches the correct place at the rear

Because the feet are so closely aligned when in L-Stance, the crescent described on the floor is much shallower than in the ITF Walking Stance for example.

CRESCENT METHOD

The rear foot describes an arc on the floor, moving in towards the lead foot

Halfway through the movement the feet are parallel to each other, some people touch them together at this point

The foot continues to describe the arc on the floor until it reaches the correct place at the front

STEPPING METHOD

The rear foot steps forward 90°

Halfway through the movement the feet are parallel to each other and one shoulder width apart

The foot continues forward until it reaches the correct place at the front

Rather than repeat a similar set of images representing how to move back, please refer to the above pictures in reverse order to understand the following instructions.

CRESCENT METHOD

1. The lead foot describes an arc on the floor, moving in towards the rear foot.

2. Halfway through the movement the feet are parallel to each other, some people touch them together at this point.

3. The foot continues to describe the arc on the floor until it reaches the correct place at the rear.

STEPPING METHOD

1. The lead foot steps forward 90°.

2. Halfway through the movement the feet are parallel to each other and one shoulder width apart.

3. The foot continues forward until it reaches the correct place at the rear

3

THE STANCES OF SAJU JIRUGI, CHON-JI AND TAEGEUK IL JANG

4

LOOKING PAST 'NEUTRAL STANCE'

Chunbi Sogi (a Ready Stance) is the start and end of every pattern within taekwondo. You move from Chunbi into the appropriate Ready Stance and at the end of the pattern you move back into Chunbi Sogi. Often the move is made by turning to the left or right at the end of the pattern, sometimes it is made by moving backwards, as in Chon-Ji.

When analysing patterns for applications that can be used in a practical manner, many people disregard this stance as either a cultural nicety that does not apply to the street, or disregard the stance as not being practical.

During my research I have found Chunbi Sogi to be a hidden gem, just like I have with Walking Stance. In this chapter I shall show you some possible applications and list the predictive responses caused by the actions.

Defender being grabbed by lapels

APPLICATION

No-one will grab you with extended arms unless they're trying to push back towards a wall for example. Even then they are very unlikely to use a stiff arm. It is not a natural thing for people to do. If they are grabbing you, and it is with both hands, it is most likely that they are intending to pull you forward, headbutt you, or slam you against an object behind you. The latter is usually done by pulling you forward initially to take your balance, and then reversing the motion.

The first 'good' thing about this form of attack is that both hands of the attacker are committed to holding on to you and therefore aren't free to cause you any further damage. Their mindset is also committed to holding on to you (prior to following through with the next part of the attack if any). In Ed Parker's art of Kenpo Karate this is termed as a 'Gift'. Simply put, they have now cut down their attack options to a limited set. These options are usually limited to the knee, stamp, push or slam, headbutt, or throw or they may lean in to bite you. The second good thing is that both your hands and feet are free and you are able to attack pretty much how you like. There are many things you can do from this position, but we'll just concentrate on Chunbi Sogi for the purposes of this chapter.

The attacker has grabbed
you by the lapels

Take your arms and raise them so
that your fists are palm towards you

Bring your hands up and behind their
head and then rake your fists (palms
facing you) into GB20, through and then
down and round punching back out into
either their stomach, spleen points in the
groin or into their testicles.

Pull your hands towards yourself,
almost as if you were closing
two windows, and strike in to
GB20 (which is located under the
defender's hand in the photo)

It is important that you tuck your chin in tightly to your chest to avoid being headbutted when by your attacker, either through their attack or due to your attack

Continue the strike through and then continue the motion down into their groin

LOCATION OF GB20

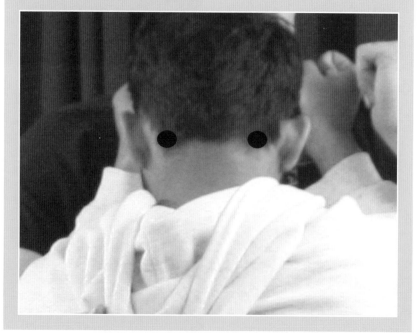

SHORT ANALYSIS

GB20 is referred to as 'Gates of Consciousness' for a good reason. A strong strike to this point hurts. A hard strike to this point can indeed knock someone clean out and a very strong strike to this point can possibly seriously injure them. Whatever the strength of the strike, it should pull their head down and towards you. This then allows you to use your shoulder or head to strike into their face as their head comes forward. They may well rise up onto their toes for a second or two. Their grip could also be loosened and depending on the strength of the strike, they might move their hands to the affected area. The lower strikes will cause them to bend forward from the hips whilst moving back. If the strike is hard enough they will release you in order to move their hands to the affected area.

The first double strike could well be the only strike you need in order to get them to release you (the whole point of the technique after all). The follow-up double strike can be debilitating and will facilitate getting the release you need in order to escape or follow-up.

This technique will most likely require a follow-up in order to finish the fight, and there are many options as to how to do this throughout the book.

CHUNBI AS A FINISHING TECHNIQUE AKA CHUNBI SWEEP

APPLICATION

Many of the techniques that were developed for Practical Taekwondo™ and Practical Self-Defence™ are designed to make escape as easy as possible. Therefore techniques were designed to either prevent the attacker from being able to follow the defender, or to impede their ability to follow the defender as much as possible. Because it was important that the techniques be as accessible as possible, it became clear that getting the attacker onto the floor (whilst the defender retained their own vertical position) as quickly as possible was the best solution.

As a result of coming to this conclusion it was decided that throws were too technical to learn quickly (especially in a self-defence context where you often have a *very* limited time frame to teach attendees useful skills, ranging from a half-day seminar to a few one-hour lessons for a number of weeks) and both hands are tied up. It was therefore decided to examine takedowns, sweeps and buckles and it's from here that the term 'Chunbi Sweep' was coined.

In the following technique, the defender and attacker have been trading blows. Using correct technique, the defender has moved into a position where they are outside of the attacker's attacking limb and have moved their feet in close to the attacker.

The defender is to the outside of the attacker, their feet are close

The defender maintains their hold on the attacker's arm, whilst palming their head away and to the side

The defender kicks their foot forward in the direction that the attacker's lead foot is facing

Close-up of feet and the direction they are facing in

At the same time as kicking forward the defender pushes back and down with the hand on the attacker's face, moving to the chest if necessary for greater leverage

Both the kick and the push result in the attacker being taken off-balance and going to the ground. The defender can now finish as necessary

SHORT ANALYSIS

As with the Walking Stance applications there are two responses to this. The attacker is either going to go into a highly extended stance aka 'the splits', or be taken completely to the floor.

Depending on the softener you used in order to prepare them for the sweep they may or may not be in a position to get back to their feet. Either way you have a valuable opening to make your get away and you should take it.

It is important that you sweep the attacker's foot in the direction that their toes are pointing. Sweeping to the left or the right of the foot is possible, but if the attacker has based or posted their leg (put the majority of their weight onto that leg) this is made much harder. Going in the direction of the toes makes a strong sweep all the more effective.

5

PRESSURE POINTS

To say that pressure points are a contentious issue in the martial arts is somewhat of an understatement. The two main schools of thinking are that:

1. They do not work and are centred around meaningless mumbo-jumbo designed to fool people into thinking that they are learning more than they really are.

2. That they do exist, that they are valid and that they are a valuable addition to martial arts and should be studied by all.

I fall into the latter group. Unfortunately, there are a number of schools of thought amongst the supporters of pressure points.

1. The first group uses the terminology of Traditional Chinese Medicine (TCM) coupled with the 'Destructive Cycle'. This group believes that not only do pressure points follow the meridians specified by TCM, but that they also correspond to the five elements of Fire, Water, Wood, Earth and Metal.

    Used in conjunction with each other these points are believed to enhance the effects of the pressure points. Fire points, for example, are effective when employed with Wood points (fire burns wood). As you can see, it can get very complicated very quickly – especially when you bring colours (including what you're wearing), element stances and sounds into the mix.

2. The second group uses Western Medicine's (WM) thought process. In a nutshell this boils down to the fact that yes, pressure points work, but we are not entirely sure why. They use Western Medical terms to refer to the location of the points. Unfortunately this means that you not only have to learn the locations of all of the pressure points, but also the names of the bones and the muscles around which they are located.

3. The third group believes in a much simpler system pioneered by pressure points master Professor Rick Clark. They have reduced pressure points usage to the simple system of 'Just Hit Here' (JHH). In other words, they know where the points are, how to hit them and what happens when they do hit them. They do not bother with any fancy terminology nor in-depth explanations as to how and why pressure points work.

For the purposes of this book I am going to use the terminology of TCM with Professor Clark's system of JHH. I do this because using the terminology of TCM, for example, GB20 (Gall Bladder 20) allows people to refer to a specific point rather than saying 'the point on the back of the head'. It is an easy system to learn if you just stick to the point naming and allows you to train in pressure points without having to bother with all the in-depth explanations and terminology required by TCM or WM.

Unfortunately, mainstream taekwondo schools do not teach pressure points specifically. They do mostly have a list of vulnerable areas but they are not referred to as pressure points.

Areas targeted are usually grouped into the three sections, high, middle and low and usually consist of:

- eyes
- nose
- jaw (point)
- jaw (hinge)
- neck
- base of skull
- philtrum

- throat
- temple
- solar plexus
- heart
- kidneys
- chest
- stomach
- armpit
- ribs
- collar bone
- back
- groin
- coccyx
- knee
- shin
- instep
- achilles tendon

As you can see they list the more common places such as the eyes, the groin and the kidneys. However, they also have the philtrum (located on the middle of the top lip, just beneath the septum of the nose) and the base of the neck. Both of these are in fact pressure points.

The philtrum is an extremely painful place to be hit and doing so can induce dizziness, nausea and cause the eyes to water copiously. Back Fists and knuckle raps are particularly effective at striking this area.

PRESSURE POINTS ARE A BONUS

Another important thing to remember is that you should never view pressure points as the be-all-and-end-all. Correct technique delivered in an accurate and forceful manner is vital to winning any fight.

Pressure points should be viewed as a bonus. To use an analogy by Professor Rick Clark, your delivery system is like an arrow, with pressure points being poison added to the tip. What he means by this is that if you get hit by an arrow you are most likely going to be killed by the arrow itself. The poison is there to help you along just in case you are not killed.

Do not aim specifically for pressure points. Deliver a strike to an area you know contains pressure points, but do not try to go for a specific point and specific response. There is no guarantee that you will hit the point and no guarantee that the person being hit will respond in the way you require.

Although a degree of accuracy is required to hit *specific* pressure points, there are a large number of pressure points located on the body and they are often close to each other.

If you look at the Image below you will see that although pressure points themselves are small, the area of response is roughly the size of a new ten pence piece. By this I mean that if you hit in that area you will have some (not all) of the benefit of a pressure point strike.

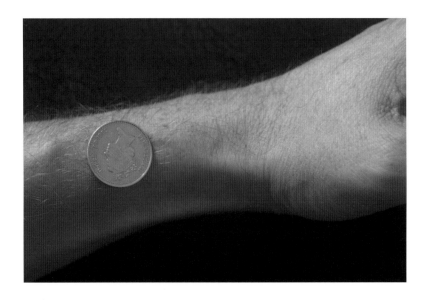

Taking this further it therefore makes sense to strike in areas where there are clusters of points. This not only lessens the chances of you missing a point altogether, but increases the effect felt by the attacker.

As you can see on the side of the neck and the jaw, there are a number of pressure points grouped closely together. This obviously makes these areas highly vulnerable to attack.

NOTE: ALL OF THE POINTS SHOWN ARE MIRRORED ON THE OTHER SIDE

The points used in Practical Taekwondo™ are listed below. Not every point on the body is listed, nor do the applications hit every point, every time. Please note that the pressure points are mirrored on both sides of the body. For simplicity's sake I have only shown them on one side each.

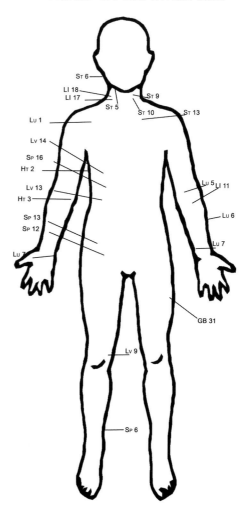

6

THE BURGAR RATING SYSTEM (BRS)

BURGAR'S CRITERIA

Bill Burgar is not someone most taekwondo practitioners will have heard of. This is mainly because he is a karate practitioner. Bill has done what very few people in modern martial arts do today. He spent five years looking at *one* pattern and seeing how he could apply the moves in a street self-defence situation. When he found a technique he then scored it using an excellent measuring system to see if it actually was practical for use on the street. Aside from designing an effective rating system, he also wrote an amazing book that chronicled not only his journey through the techniques, but also his thought processes and how he arrived at the stunning the conclusion he did. *Five Years One Kata* is available from *all* good bookstores.

FIVE YEARS ONE KATA

Bill Burgar

This remarkable book gives the reader a unique insight into an amazing five-year study of a single kata (Gojushiho). It shows the depth that is waiting to be discovered by the close study of kata, covering an incredible range of subjects including:

- imagery
- the psychology of confrontation
- the common acts of physical violence
- vital points and how to exploit them
- the methodology for the break-down and understanding of kata
- the applications of the kata
- the principles of karate and how to apply them
- the applications (in detail) for each of the movements of Gojushiho
- the major variations of each application
- objective measurements regarding their practicality
- how to link the applications together

The author also explains how to undertake your own study using a single kata of your choice, and how to build a training regime based on the kata. If you have ever wondered what kata is really all about then this book is for you.

The criteria he used to score the techniques are listed below.

- Proactive
- Keeps Initiative
- Maximises Safety
- Maximises Redundancy
- Workable with adrenaline
- Works with instinct
- Maximises Predictable Response
- Unbalances the Attacker

- Leads the mind of the Attacker

- Low Maintenance

- Range

- Simple

- Transferable Skills

- Overall Balance of Pattern

PROACTIVE

The scale goes from total reaction through to pre-emption. The nearer you are to the pre-emption end of the scale the better chance you have of maintaining control.

The nearer you are to the reactive end of the scale the more you need to examine the application and see if it puts you in a position to be proactive. The nearer the application is to being reactive, the lower the score gets.

KEEPS INITIATIVE

The technique must ensure that the attacker can't assert any control. This is coupled with pro-activeness but is applied at the end of the application to see how easy it is to flow into another proactive application.

If the application leaves you off-balanced and poorly positioned to continue being proactive it scores lower. If you can keep striking the attacker and keeping them both on the defensive and on the back foot, it scores higher.

MAXIMISES SAFETY

Fights aren't safe but there are good and bad places to be in during a fight. Being out of range is 'safe', being on the outside is 'safe' and off-balancing them is 'safe'.

However, in order to ensure we are damaging the attacker we must take some risk, for example, closing the distance in order to strike them.

MAXIMISES REDUNDANCY

Applications must have built-in fail-safes so that if one part of an application doesn't work the other aspects still cause the attacker problems (such as pain, injury, distraction, or unbalancing).

WORKABLE WITH ADRENALINE

Tunnel vision (often seen as a 'stare', or 'giving someone the eye', and which focuses your attention on your attacker, but also limits your peripheral vision), auditory exclusion (the loss of hearing), the loss of complex motor skills (the inability to perform highly technical applications for example), lack of ability to think clearly, muscle spasm (the shakes), instability in the lower limbs, and so on, are all signs of an adrenal dump. Therefore applications need to be able to work with these. Anything that relies on being able to see to the side or behind will score lower as would anything that required fine motor skills for example.

WORKS WITH INSTINCT

When you go into autopilot you tend to do what comes naturally rather than what you've trained for (unless you have trained that specific technique at least a few hundred times in a concentrated time span). If you can marry instinct and application you have a better chance of performing the application as you've trained it.

MAXIMISES PREDICTABLE RESPONSE

This is my favourite due to my Kempo background. Kick a man in the groin and there are certain things he will do, such as moving his head forwards and his pelvis back (even if you miss, they will be doing this to get out of the way). Their hands will also move down towards the area, either to ward the incoming blow or to grab the affected area. The more reliable a predictive response you get the higher this scores on the measure.

UNBALANCES THE ATTACKER

Unbalancing sets us up to keep the initiative using our proactive techniques, or ideally to just run away. If an application leaves the attacker perfectly balanced, it obviously scores lowly.

LEADS THE MIND OF THE ATTACKER

Any action that makes the attacker think about anything but attacking scores highly. One tactic might be to ask them what the time is. Whilst their brain is processing the question (and possibly looking for an answer), you have the opportunity to counter-attack them.

LOW MAINTENANCE

If an application requires very little practice in order to keep it at a workable level it scores highly. These are usually the simple, brutal techniques that are most natural in execution and easily visualised, for example an eye gouge.

RANGE REALISTIC

Does the application work within a realistic range (rather than kicking range for example) and deal with Habitual Acts Of Violence (HAOV)? This scores higher.

HABITUAL ACTS OF VIOLENCE (HAOV)

Put simply, HAOV are the most common form of attacks that you are most likely to face in your area or country.

One area, for example, might see a high amount of swinging punches being thrown, another might see headbutts being a common way of attacking someone.

You simply need to work out what the most common threats are in your area and country and then work to counter them. Compiling the list can be difficult, but also makes for very interesting research and means that you do not waste valuable time concentrating on counters to attacks that you are unlikely to face.

SIMPLE

KISS. Keep It Simple, Stupid.

Applications should be simple to perform under stress, simple to learn, simple to maintain and simple to perform under difficult conditions (such as a slippery street). The more moves an application has, the less likely that it is going to be able to meet these requirements.

TRANSFERABLE SKILLS

The application should have skills that can be transferred to other tasks. If it does then when you are practicing the one application you are also practicing the other application. So, one defence for many attacks is going to score highly. Anything that relies on simple punches for example scores highly here.

OVERALL BALANCE OF PATTERN

This is based on whether you're studying one pattern exclusively. In most modern patterns, analysis of applications is usually considered in isolation to the rest of the pattern and can give an uneven distribution of defensive techniques. For example, there may be a lot of defences against lapel grabs and swinging punches. Although they might be valid techniques you'll get log-jam if you practice them all.

6 SCORING

When scoring applications it does not matter whether you use the Burgar Rating System as outlined below, or a numeric system. If you do use a numeric system (decimal for example), then you are still going to have to define what is a 'bad' score compared to an 'excellent' score.

VERY BAD

The first thing you need to do with this is ditch it. That is also the last thing you need to do.

BAD

This is not what you want to have as an application score. However, there are many 'martial arts' applications that actually score this. This is due to the way martial arts have become disassociated from true 'fighting arts' and have become 'ways'. As soon as you remove the need to be practical from the equation, all manner of moves can be devised.

GOOD

Although this is not excellent, it does not mean that the application does not have its merits and that it cannot be used practically.

VERY GOOD

This is where all of your hard work is starting to pay off. You have an application that you can drill well, that comes to you instinctively, is simple to learn and maintain and which does the job.

EXCELLENT

There is no doubt whatsoever as to the effectiveness of the application. This application covers all the bases and, all being well, ensures that your attacker is neutralised as quickly and as safely as possible.

PUTTING THE SYSTEM INTO PRACTICE

Now that you have an understanding as to how the system works we shall look at two applications. One will rate highly according to the criteria, and one shall rate badly, deliberately so.

It is important to bear in mind, however, that what might work for one person, might not necessarily work for another. This means that something you personally score as very bad, might well be something that someone else is more than comfortable using and has done so successfully. The applications demonstrated within the book are ones that I felt comfortable with at the time of writing. However, you must never allow yourself to stagnate and should try to find better, faster and more effective applications.

FIRST APPLICATION

The first application is one that is taken directly from the movements of Saju Jirugi. For the purpose of the demonstration the punch is being thrown using their right hand.

PROACTIVE

This technique is not proactive. It relies on the attacker initiating the attack and in a certain, albeit very common, manner.

RATING: Bad

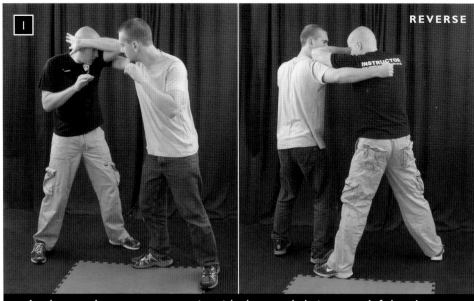

As the attacker starts to step in with the punch, bring your left hand up to your right shoulder. This will effectively cover your face and head.

Step your left leg forward, keeping your left elbow pointed towards the right-hand side of the attacker. Keep your right hand up in a guard position to block any left-handed blocks that may be following this.

3

As soon as their blow makes contact with your elbow or arm, strike outward and downwards (as if performing a Hammer Fist strike turning into Low Block)

4

Continue the motion of your left hand and attempt to grab or trap their right arm, preferably around the upper forearm or shoulder. It does not matter if this misses however.

6

THE BURGAR RATING SYSTEM (BRS)

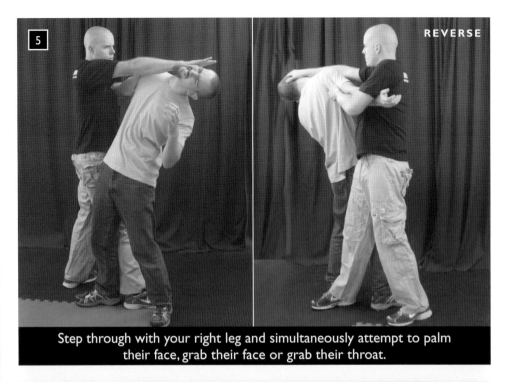

Step through with your right leg and simultaneously attempt to palm their face, grab their face or grab their throat.

Continue to turn to the left, using the trapped arm to pull them down and your right hand to push in the same direction

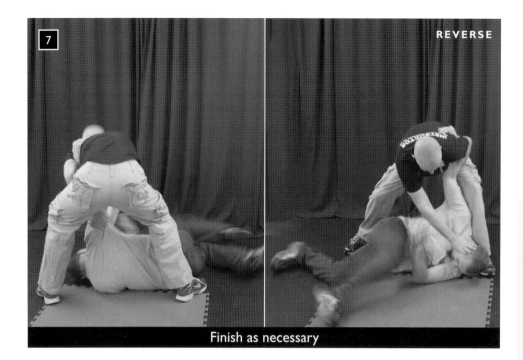

REVERSE

Finish as necessary

KEEPS INITIATIVE

Although the initiative initially rests with the attacker, the defender rapidly regains the initiative and maintains it. By stepping in towards the attacker the defender is also rapidly changing their mindset from being the defender to being the attacker. Similarly, the attacker also has to undergo a mindset change from attacker to defender.

RATING: Very Good

MAXIMISES SAFETY

Although moving to the outside of an attacker is the best thing the defender can do, the attack means that doing so is very difficult. Moving in towards the attacker closes down their ability to throw more full-power punches, limits any kicking techniques that they might have thrown had the defender moved away from the initial punch. The head and face are well-covered by the left and right arms, ensuring that any blow that lands will be smothered by them.

RATING: Excellent

MAXIMISES REDUNDANCY

Regardless as to whether the elbow actually makes contact with their arm, the defender's head is still covered.

Regardless as to whether the right punch is actually landed, it is still in a position to unbalance the attacker and aid in the takedown.

Regardless as to whether the defender is able to take the attacker down to the floor, they are still in a good position to move to a barrage of punches, Elbows and knees.

RATING: Excellent

WORKABLE WITH ADRENALINE

There is nothing here that is difficult to perform. All the strikes can be thrown as club-like attacks if necessary and the initial cover is a simple flinch when all is said and done. There are no fine motor skills required nor are mental gymnastics a feature.

RATING: Excellent

WORKS WITH INSTINCT

The initial block is really a flinch. Unlike martial artists who have had flinches trained out of them, normal people will protect their head and face by raising their hands in front of them. Therefore the covering block works with, rather than against, instinct.

RATING: Excellent

MAXIMISES PREDICTABLE RESPONSE

If the elbow connects with any part of the attacker's arm it will not only smother the blow, but it will also cause the arm to bounce off and, if it hits a pressure point, may well 'kill' the arm, causing it to drop to the side. This will also cause the attacker's head to turn to the right, opening up and stretching the neck.

Whether or not it does 'kill' the arm, the elbow, coupled with the stepping in, will unbalance the attacker and cause them to move slightly backward, allowing you to step further in the second time. All of this gives you more time to get your counter-punch in and to attempt the takedown if you deem it necessary.

RATING: Excellent

UNBALANCES THE ATTACKER

As demonstrated above, the attacker will be taken off-balance by your initial block and step in. The follow-up punch can go past the attacker if necessary and the defender's upper arm can be used to barge the attacker back and over.

The final move of the application is actually a throw which, if successful, will take the attacker to the floor, completely destroying their balance.

RATING: Excellent

LEADS THE MIND OF THE ATTACKER

The application leads the mind of the attacker in more ways than one.

The first is that the attacker is expecting to inflict pain on the defender, not have the defender inflict pain upon them immediately.

Having the defender move in close and inflict pain forces the attacker to shift his mindset from that of 'attack' to that of defend.

Finally the defender's initial defensive move, the follow-up shoulder barge and the takedown all force the attacker to concentrate on retaining their balance, rather than retaining the initiative or recommencing the attack.

RATING: Excellent

LOW MAINTENANCE

There is a flinch, a Low Block and a punch. None of these techniques need to be performed perfectly in order to work. The flinch is natural, the Low Block is simple to perform and a punch can be taught to a beginner in less than five minutes.

RATING: Excellent

RANGE

The technique works well within the range of a very common HAOV. It also starts at a realistic range rather than 'sparring' range.

RATING: Excellent

SIMPLE

There is nothing difficult to either remember or perform here. Whether the application is performed with dojang-perfect technique, or as a windmill of flailing arms and hands, the application contains techniques that are taught to beginners the world over.

RATING: Excellent

TRANSFERABLE SKILLS

The Low Block is found in a number of low-level patterns and the student will be performing it for many months. Therefore it is going to be one of the more instinctive and ingrained techniques in the syllabus.

A punch is a punch. Taekwondo is a striking art that utilises the punch greatly.

RATING: Excellent

OVERALL BALANCE OF PATTERN

Saju Jirugi, Chon-Ji and Taegeuk Il Jang (to a slightly lesser amount) are simple-to-perform patterns that are remarkably effective and which usually leave the attacker on the floor after a barrage of blows.

RATING: Excellent

The application described is clearly an effective application containing simple-to-use and simple-to-learn techniques that will quickly become ingrained into the student's psyche.

The following technique is designed to show how a poorly thought out technique can be a complete waste of time. Unfortunately this example is one that is currently used in a number of books. Although not found in the patterns contained within this book, it is an excellent example of badly thought through applications.

Showing this application with the defender in a dobok actually makes it 'look' a lot more reasonable, which is why I have demonstrated the technique in street clothing, as it makes both the block itself and the application of the block, all the more ridiculous.

APPLICATION

The defender is being attacked by two attackers at the same time. The attacker on the right attacks with a punch; at the same time the attacker on the left attacks with a kick. Staying rooted in Ready Stance, the defender blocks both attacks at the same time with a Scissor Block.

PROACTIVE

This technique is not proactive. It also relies on the attackers initiating the attack simultaneously.

RATING: Very Bad

KEEPS INITIATIVE

The initiative starts with the attacker and remains with the attacker. Neither block takes the attacker off-balance sufficiently, nor does the defender place himself in a position that allows them to take the fight to the attacker.

RATING: Very Bad

MAXIMISES SAFETY

The defender stays in front of both attackers. Neither block deflects them sufficiently to alter their path of attack, nor does it take the fight to them or allow the defender to move out of range of either attacker.

The head and main torso are completely open to any follow-up attack that might be thrown.

RATING: Very Bad

MAXIMISES REDUNDANCY

If either block fails the defender is going to be hit. There is no back-up as they are totally committed to blocking both attacks. Once one attack gets through, the other attacker will have little difficulty rejoining the fight.

RATING: Very Bad

WORKABLE WITH ADRENALINE

Blocking two attacks from two different directions and two different attackers whilst under the influence of a good dose of fear is going to be nearly impossible.

RATING: Very Bad

WORKS WITH INSTINCT

The defender stays rooted to the spot in an unnatural pose. The blocks are flinch-like but only when used on their own.

RATING: Very Bad

MAXIMISES PREDICTABLE RESPONSE

Because both blocks are being delivered at the same time, neither will be delivered with sufficient force to 'kill' the attacking limb. Neither attacker will be sufficiently deviated from their path of attack and the blocks do not lend themselves to follow-up attacks.

RATING: Very Bad

UNBALANCES THE ATTACKER

The Lower Block may well unbalance the kicking attacker, but this is unlikely.

RATING: Very Bad

LEADS THE MIND OF THE ATTACKER

Unfortunately the attackers will not find themselves sufficiently distracted by either block. The block against the punch leaves the attacker able to hit with the other hand with little difficulty. The block against the kick leaves the attacker still standing and able to follow up with any hand strikes they deem necessary.

RATING: Very Bad

LOW MAINTENANCE

This needs to be practised on a regular basis in order to drill it so that it becomes 'instinctive'.

RATING: Very Bad

RANGE

This starts within an unrealistic distance.

RATING: Very Bad

SIMPLE

Although the two techniques are simple to perform when isolated, there is nothing simple about performing the two of them at the same time against two attackers.

RATING: Very Bad

TRANSFERABLE SKILLS

The Low Block and Inner Forearm Block are found throughout taekwondo, however performing them simultaneously is not. This technique is much better placed to be used against a different attack.

RATING: Very Bad

OVERALL BALANCE OF PATTERN

This technique is not found in any of the other early patterns and your time would be much better spent elsewhere.

RATING: Very Bad

As you can see, the overall rating for this technique is Very Bad. It's appalling that techniques such as this are taught as being valid defences when they are most certainly not.

7

HOW TO PERFORM THE BLOCKS

Blocking is an important part of any martial art. Saju Jirugi, Chon-Ji and Taegeuk Il Jang use a number of basic blocks that, on the whole, work well with instinct. Indeed it could be argued that because of this, the earlier patterns are the most effective.

The blocks we shall cover in this chapter are:

- Low Block

- Rising Block

- Inward Outer Forearm Block/Inside Block

- Outward Inner Forearm Block/ Outside Block

THE LOW BLOCK

The Down Block, Low Block, Lower Outer Forearm Block, Najunde Bakat Palmok Makgi, Arae Makgi or Gedan Barai is one of the first blocks taught to many beginner martial artists. For those practising ITF taekwondo it is a core part of their training for their first two belts.

As with any technique there is more than one way to perform the block. In this book we shall look at two of the ways, Hip Twist (with a high chamber) and the WTF/Karate Method.

For those students doing the sine wave, using either of these methods in your self-defence applications, such as one-step, should not prove to be a problem as they will prove to be much quicker and more flexible than if you were to try to use the sine wave.

THE HIP TWIST

The Hip Twist is the method that was taught before the introduction of and concentration on, the sine wave. In isolation it does not make sense to chamber a block this high and with both hands to the side of your head, however research has shown that there are definitely a number of techniques and applications that can be used with this method as you shall see later on in the book.

For those that turn their block hand out (a natural 'mistake' to make whilst still a novice) remember the maxim of 'inside out, outside in'. This means that if you are performing an Inner Forearm Block the blocking arm goes on the outside of the cross, and if you are performing an Outer Forearm Block, the blocking hand goes on the inside of the cross.

For demonstration purposes we shall show the block being performed in a static ITF Walking Stance/WTF Front Stance. The student is performing a left Low Block and is already in left Walking Stance.

The student is in left Walking Stance

The student brings their left hand across their body

As you can see it appears that the student is trying to hold their ear. At the same time as the left hand comes across the right hand comes straight up and goes back-to-back with the left hand. Note how the upper body of the student is twisted to the right; this adds to the speed and power of the block when they unwind.

As you can see the hands are now crossed

7

HOW TO PERFORM THE BLOCKS

5

From there the student performs the block with the left hand cutting across the body and the right hand returning to the right hip

WTF/KARATE METHOD

The reason that this book refers to Area Makgi as the 'WTF/Karate Method' is because the motion used to perform this block is practically identical in both arts.

For demonstration purposes we shall show the block being performed in a static ITF Walking Stance/WTF Front Stance. The student is performing a left Low Block and is already in left Walking Stance.

Whilst it is obvious that the Hip Twist Method is a more defensive, grabbing technique, the WTF/Karate Method is much more offensive in nature. It not only deals with the incoming attack, but immediately goes on the offensive to regain the initiative.

The student is in left
Walking Stance

The student brings their left hand
across their body

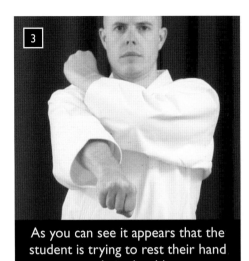

As you can see it appears that the student is trying to rest their hand on their shoulder

At the same time as the left hand comes across the right hand comes straight out and down, as if performing a punch

As soon as the hands have chambered the left hand cuts back across the body and the right hand returns to the right hip

ITF INWARD OUTER FOREARM BLOCK – WTF INSIDE BLOCK

This block is best used to deflect straight attacks coming towards either the body or head. Fortunately both the ITF and WTF use *similar* methods for chambering this block.

The student brings their left hand up to the side of their head

The hand is then brought across the body just past the centreline

The ITF and WTF versions of this block vary enough that we will detail the two.

THE HIP TWIST METHOD

The positioning of the hands chamber for the Hip Twist Method is exactly the same as for Low Block, however the place it is chambered from is the hips.

The left hand comes across the body and rests on the right hand

Note how the hands are crossed at the hip

The left hand now comes out and up, stopping just above the head with the arm at a 45° angle

THE WTF METHOD

As with the WTF Method of chambering the Low Block, the non-blocking hand can be used to counter-punch or grab.

1

The left hand comes across the body to the right hip. At the same time the right hand is raised so that the right arm is above the left

2

The left hand now comes out and up, stopping just above the head with the arm at a 45° angle

THE HIP TWIST METHOD

For the Inner Forearm Block, the position of the hands in the chamber is the direct opposite to that of the Low Block. Another difference to note is that the palms of both hands face away from the defender's ears.

7

HOW TO PERFORM THE BLOCKS

1

The left hand comes across the body whilst the right hand comes up to ear height

7

Note how the hands are positioned with the blocking hand on the outside of the cross

The left hand now comes back across the body whilst the right hand returns to the hip

THE WTF METHOD

The position for this block is exactly the same as for the Rising Block.

The left hand comes across the body to the right hip

At the same time the right hand is raised so that the right arm is above the left

3

The left hand now comes back across the body whilst the right hand returns to the hip

8

LOOKING PAST THE 'BLOCK'

What is a block when it's not a block? Anything you want it to be!

On a more serious note, defining a technique as one thing limits it to being just that and closes your mind's eye to the opportunities that such techniques can offer beyond simply stopping a certain attack.

There is much more to the Low Block, the Inward Outer Forearm Block, the Outward Inner Forearm Block and the Rising Block than what they are normally used for. Unfortunately 'blocks' tend to be taken at face value with the result that people fail to see how they might be used to strike, check and choke their attackers for example. In this chapter you will be introduced to some of the many ways that they can be used. Other than to 'block' that is.

THE LOW BLOCK

As outlined in the previous chapter, the Low Block is probably the first block that anyone beginning taekwondo will use. Most will be told that it is to be used solely against kicks, usually in ITF Walking Stance/WTF Front Stance.

Research has shown that, aside from middle or high Outer Forearm Block, this is one of the most versatile and powerful techniques taught to lower belts and indeed is so versatile that Professor Rick Clark of the Ao Denkou Kai has written a very successful book titled *75 Down Blocks*.

Aside from being easy for beginners to perform, this block relies very little on good technique to be powerful, although this does of course help. Generally performed in Walking Stance/Front Stance during patterns, it can easily be applied in virtually any stance

Low Block

The following applications are ones that research has discovered in Saju Jirugi, the first exercise taught to beginners in the ITF; Chon Ji, the first pattern taught to ninth Kup in the ITF and Taegeuk Il Jang, the first pattern taught within the WTF. Please assume that unless stated otherwise, the attack is always right-handed. This is purely because this book is using Pareto's 80/20 rule which states that you are most likely to meet the most common attacks 80 per cent of the time. Therefore, 80 per cent of the attacks that you face are most likely to be right-handed.

We have detailed two different methods of how to perform the Low Block so will now explore the other ways that the Low Block can be used.

The Low Block is not a technique which requires a high amount of skill to perform well, which is most likely why it is the first block to be taught to beginners. Similarly many of the techniques that can be used as alternative applications also lack the need for technical excellence.

Forearm Strike

The Forearm Strike or Smash is, to put it bluntly, a clubbing technique. It can be performed by a beginner on their first night within five to ten minutes. There are basically two different types of Forearm Strike: the Inward Outer Forearm and the Outward Outer Forearm. Obviously they can be delivered on a number of different planes but it boils down to just two strikes.

You might think that the Inward Outer Forearm Strike does not belong, but it does if you are using the WTF/Karate method of Low Block. The inward strike is performed by the hand that is 'blocking', the strike occurs whilst the hand is travelling to the opposite shoulder, it is just unfortunate that there is an attacker in its way.

INWARD OUTER FOREARM TO
OUTWARD OUTER FOREARM STRIKE

INWARD OUTER FOREARM TO
OUTWARD OUTER FOREARM STRIKE

8

LOOKING PAST THE 'BLOCK'

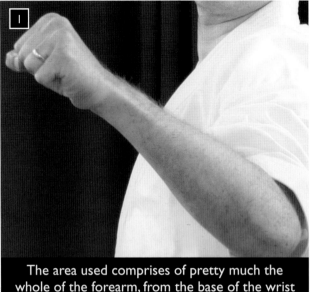

The area used comprises of pretty much the
whole of the forearm, from the base of the wrist
to about 3 inches up from the tip of the elbow

The defender has a high guard whilst the attacker is trying to
intimidate them by invading their space and poking them

The defender smashes their arm into the attacker's, raking towards themselves so that the arm is forced down and across the attacker's body. This makes it harder for the attacker to counter-punch

The defender immediately reverses the motion of their hand and performs an Outward Outer Forearm Strike to the attacker's neck on the left-hand side whilst stepping or shuffling forward with the left leg

Note how the defender's right hand is able to check the attacker's left hand, allowing the strike to go in

As you can see, a large portion of the forearm can be used to hit a number of points on the attacker's neck

SHORT ANALYSIS

As with any poking or jabbing movement, catching them at the right time can be difficult. This is the sort of 'attack' that is repeated, and usually repeated in some form of sequence. Once the sequence has been started the application is short and to the point.

The first strike clears the offending arm out of the way and gives the defender the initiative, whilst the second strike allows the defender to hit a vulnerable area. Because this is a 'flailing' technique, whether the defender hits the neck points or not is irrelevant as the next most likely target to be hit will be the jaw line or face of the attacker. The result will still be a stunning attack which will allow the defender to continue their attack if necessary.

ELBOW (USING THE 'ITF' CHAMBER)

If we take a look at the Thai Fighter we see similarities between his Elbow and the chamber and indeed the actual movement of the arms is also very similar. Breaking it down we can see how the taekwondo fighter can perform a parry, trap and Elbow whilst entering the chamber.

Left hand parries the incoming attack

Right hand grabs attacking arm

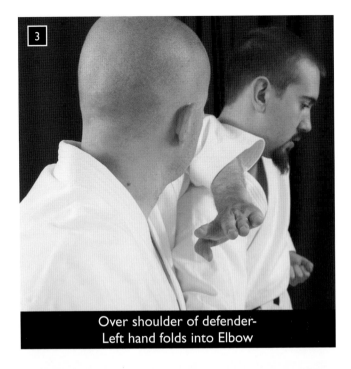

Over shoulder of defender–
Left hand folds into Elbow

Right hand returns to hip, pulling the attacker
sharply forward and down

Left hand comes out into Low Block,
striking the attacker

The hand continues so that it is across
the attacker's chest

The defender then performs Chunbi Sweep

SHORT ANALYSIS

As with the previous technique this is best done against an intimidation technique such as jabbing finger, repeated pushes, and so on. The technique not only takes the initiative from the attacker but also takes the defender from being a passive target straight through to physical confrontation, and immediately puts the attacker onto their back foot mentally.

Already stunned by the Elbow, the attacker will find the sharp yank forward and down even more disorientating. The step forward also adds momentum to the second strike and places the attacker in a good position for a sweep. The sweep to the floor allows the defender to leave the scene better than if the attacker was still standing.

SIMULTANEOUS PARRY AND COUNTER-PUNCH (USING THE 'WTF' CHAMBER)

The WTF/Karate Method is a much more aggressive and offensive manoeuvre. Rather than parrying and then counter-attacking as in the Hip Twist Method, the WTF/Karate Method takes the fight to attacker from the off. Not only are you going to be counter-punching them, but you will also be stepping to their outside and into a position of advantage from the start.

The attacker comes in with a straight arm attack, for simplicity this will be a straight punch, but this could also be a Palm Heel, a push or a grab.
The defender steps forward 45° to the outside of the attack bringing their left hand across to the right shoulder, parrying the attack on the way. At the same time, they punch down into the attacker's stomach. Note that this does not have to be a punch but could just be stopping motion

The defender then finishes the Low Block
by striking the attacker

The defender then sweeps the attacker
to the floor

SHORT ANALYSIS

This is a reactive rather than proactive application that relies on an attack coming in on a specific plane. Positioning of the hands can help 'feed' such an attack by preventing other forms of attack. It works with the instinctive need to cover the face in the event of attack coupled with the 'pushing away of the attacker'.

The attacker's mindset is rapidly changed from attacker to defender whilst they are still attacking. That they are most likely going to be stepping in with the punch adds more power to the counter-strike. The counter-strike also helps in disrupting the attacker's mindset by hitting low and then high. The sweep to the floor allows the defender to leave the scene better than if the attacker was still standing.

This type of chamber is best used as a pre-emptive attack, especially if applied using turns as Positional Indicators, rather than 'just' turns.

PARRY AND CATCH
(USING THE 'ITF' CHAMBER)

The ITF version is more 'defensive' but gives the defender a good opportunity to decide whether a counter-strike is really called for. It also allows them to use control methods or joint attacks should they be required.

1

The attacker comes in with a straight arm attack, for simplicity this will be a straight punch, but this could also be a Palm Heel, a push or a grab. The defender steps forward 45° to the outside of the attack bringing their left hand across to the right shoulder, parrying the attack on the way

As soon as the attack is parried the left hand passes the attacking arm to the right arm which secures a firm hold

The attacker's right hand is then retained whilst the defender uses the Low Block to smash into the attacker's ribs

4

The defender then sweeps the attacker
to the floor

SHORT ANALYSIS

This technique requires more skill and coordination to perform and so it is best used against a repetitive attack. Once done however, the attacker rapidly finds himself in trouble as they are yanked hard and down, hit across the face and swept to the floor.

The sweep to the floor allows the defender to leave the scene better than if the attacker was still standing.

CENTRE LOCK

The Centre Lock is one that most students are aware of, but they might just call it by another name. Performed against a cross-hand grab, this is a very easy and potentially *very* damaging technique to use.

It is important to bear in mind that the grab might not be the initial attack. In fact it is best to think of the grab as a defensive move in response to something that *you* have done to the attacker. In this case one example might be that you were attempting to grab their groin. A man's natural instinct would be to grab the offending hand as quickly as possible. This technique is a *counter* to their reaction.

The attacker has grabbed the defender's right hand in a cross-hand grab

The defender immediately places their hand over the grabbing hand

The defender then rotates their right hand down and out in a clockwise motion, aiming to get the blade of the hand onto the wrist of the attacker

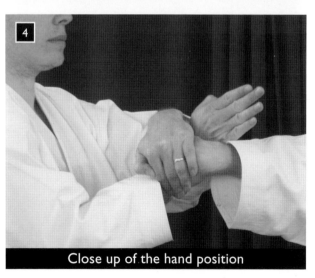

Close up of the hand position

As soon as this is done, the defender steps forward and points the index finger of the grabbed hand down and back towards their groin. Note: It is important that your hands remain as close to your body as possible and as far from the attacker's body as possible. This greatly increases the effectiveness of the technique

Breaking the attacker's wrist with the above move, the defender then finishes the attacker with the Low Block

SHORT ANALYSIS

Although this technique relies on the attacker grabbing the defender, there are a number of things that the defender can do in order to make the attacker grab. Once the grab is done the technique is very simple and very fast to perform. It works well with adrenaline and can seriously injure the attacker very quickly. Similarly, if the technique 'fails', that is, the opponent lets go as you are attempting to put the lock on, you will have still stripped your opponent's hand from yours and you are still in a position to continue your counter-attack.

Once their wrist and tendons are damaged and the attacker is on their knees reeling from the strike to the face, the defender should be able to make their getaway.

BLOCKS AS STRANGLES?

Having already demonstrated how the Low Block can be used as a percussive strike, it is time to look at how it can used to cut the attacker's blood flow off by placing pressure on their neck. *It must be borne in mind that this is a dangerous technique and should only be practiced under skilled supervision.*

The attacker has grabbed the defender by the lapels

The defender shoots forward and to the outside with the left leg. The defender then slams the left elbow into the neck of the attacker

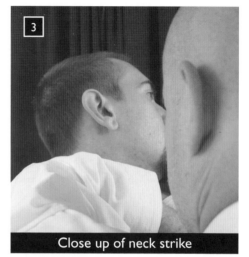

Close up of neck strike

At the same time, the defender also strikes inward with his right hand, aiming to get the knobbly bit of the wrist into the neck points on the other side. The defender immediately starts to squeeze both hands towards each other. It is perfectly alright to grab hold of the right hand to increase grip if need be

5

The defender then turns to the left violently
and takes the attacker to the floor

It should be noted that due to the area being struck the attacker may well be rendered unconscious by the first two blows. If this is the case then the defender merely allows the attacker to fall to the floor, rather than exerting more pressure.

SHORT ANALYSIS

The motion performed by the two arms mirrors the instinctive need to cover one's face when being threatened. It also serves to completely cover the head against a headbutt or strike to the head.

The step forward will have added momentum as the attacker will most likely be pulling the defender forward in order to push them backward.

The double strike to the neck is particularly effective and, even if the attacker is not knocked out, they will be stunned. This in turn will make the turn to the left and down all the more effective.

INWARD OUTER FOREARM BLOCK

The Inward Outer Forearm Block
is another clubbing block and is one
that works especially well with instinct,
alongside the Rising Block.

As well as the two techniques outlined
below, this block can also be used as
a Forearm Strike. As this has been
detailed above, it will not be covered
in this section.

HAMMER FIST

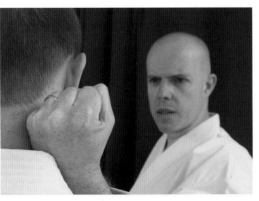

The Hammer Fist is an excellent
technique to teach beginners. This
is because anyone can be taught
to make a fist and, if you observe
children for long enough, you
will see them use the downward
hammer fist when fighting with their
peers.

The only change that you need to
make to the block is that instead of striking with the bone of the arm, you strike with
the meaty area at the bottom of your fist.

The Inward Outer Forearm Block is also a very useful tool to use when grabbed by one or both lapels. Although the blow to the arms will hurt (as it will rake down the arm points), the main objective is to trap the attacker's arms against the body long enough to counter-attack them.

The attacker has grabbed the defender by the lapels

The defender raises their hands in a 'plea' motion

The defender then smashes their left arm in to the attacker's right arm. Whilst doing this the defender tucks their chin in to avoid being accidently headbutted. Note how the attacker has stepped forward and is now leaning in towards the defender

The defender then rakes their forearm down the arms of the attacker, coming to rest at the top of their wrists/back of their hands

It is clear that the attacker is now in a position of disadvantage. This does not mean that they will remain so and a counter-attack should be performed immediately following the trap.

SHORT ANALYSIS

The smash to the right arm of the attacker not only hurts as it tracks down a number of pressure points, but it also takes their height (by dropping them down) and disrupts their balance by pulling them sharply forward.

Secondly, the technique will also cause them to open up their neck points, allowing for further strikes if necessary.

The Rising Block is really one of the most instinctive warding motions that people use. Aside from the use outlined below, the Rising Block is very good for Forearm Strikes to vulnerable points such as the neck (resembling an Upward Outward Outer Forearm Strike), as an Uppercut and as a Shovel Hook.

'BREAKING'

The direction and angle that the Rising Block takes to reach its end position makes it a very useful weapon against an attacker's arm, specifically the Elbow.

The attacker has grabbed the defender's right lapel. Note how the attacker's arm is bent at this time, this is not a 'Zombie' attack

The defender pins the grabbing hand with their right hand whilst sharply twisting their body and stepping back. This brings the attacker forward but also straightens their arm

The defender now takes their left arm starts to perform the Rising Block, going through the attacker's elbow to do so

As the defender performs the block, they snap their right hand down to their hip maintaining a strong hold on the attacker's arm

The defender then performs the Chunbi Sweep, taking the attacker to the floor

ATTACK OF THE ZOMBIES

There are many martial arts instructors that teach defences against grabs to the chest or the neck. Unfortunately, many of these scenarios require the attacker to grab the defender in an unrealistic manner. This involves the attacker performing the attack with their arms locked out, just like a zombie. This then allows the defender to use attacks such as Palm Heels to the bottom of the elbows, in order to escape.

Attackers do not attack this way. Grabs and strangles will be applied with bent arms, allowing the attacker to get the maximum leverage required.

SHORT ANALYSIS

Although this is a reactive rather than proactive application, it works well with instinctive nature. It is natural for someone who has been grabbed to pull back and away.

The backward movement enables the defender to straighten the attacker's arm whilst affecting their mindset, changing it from grabber to grabbed. The Rising Block then allows the defender to injure the attacker's arm before rapidly taking them to the ground.

Because of the way that this block is performed, it is actually a very weak technique when being used as a trapping or breaking movement. The main reason for this is that you can only rotate your elbow so far before you put yourself into an uncomfortable and possibly compromising position.

It does however lend itself to quick strikes to vulnerable points. The two ways that this book will cover are as a Thumb Fist and a Back Fist.

THUMB FIST

The Thumb Fist is a slightly exotic weapon but useful nonetheless.

To make a Thumb Fist curl your fingers as you would normally for a fist

Then place your thumb on the top of the fist and bend it

Image of the striking area

The attacker has stated his intent to do harm to the defender

The defender is in a high guard and snaps out their fist, striking in to the attacker's neck. – Note how the striking position is exactly that of the Inner Forearm Block

It is very important that the strike is flicked out and retracted as quickly as possible

Because this application is a sole strike, the Short Analysis is not applicable.

As with the Thumb Fist, the Back Fist is snapped out and back. This time however the striking area is the back of your first two knuckles but do not let this limit you. If you have to strike with the whole of the fist do so.

This is the ideal striking area

The defender is in a high guard and snaps out their Back Fist

The target is either the jaw line or the neck

As soon as the strike has landed the defender retracts it back into the high guard, or chambers for another strike

Because this application is a sole strike, the Short Analysis is not applicable.

9

LOOKING PAST THE 'PUNCH'

'Traditional' punches are taught to be delivered with the fist horizontal and with the first two knuckles on the hand being used as the impact area. This is regardless as to the actual type of punch being used, that is, Jab, Cross, Hook or Uppercut.

This is not the only way to deliver a punch however. As you can see from the pictures below, positioning of the hand can enable you to deliver a punch that is far more effective for the target being struck, and also find a good compromise between personal preference and effectiveness.

The traditional punch is delivered with the palm down and the fist on a horizontal plane.

Other styles use a 45 twist to the punch, almost as if they were holding a steering wheel.

The last most common variation is the vertical fist. In this the top two knuckles are used to strike and the fist is inclined towards the target in order to align the wrist with the rest of the arm.

In the three patterns covered in this book there are only two punches used, the obverse (same side) and reverse (opposite side) punches. These two can themselves be interpreted to cover the Jab and the Cross as well. The latter two punches are much better suited to the 'reality-based self-defence' techniques.

As you can see from the list above, there are other techniques contained within the patterns that allow the user to introduce additional punches into their training. The two techniques that we shall add to the punching repertoire in this book are the Low Block and the Rising Block.

The Low Block allows you to add the outward Hammer Fist and (with a little tweaking) the Back Fist. The Rising Block allows you to add Uppercuts and Shovel Hooks.

It is obvious that just by re-examining two 'blocks' you can add four more techniques to your armoury, whilst at the same time expanding your list of applications.

The defender has taken his attacker's balance and
has him bent backward

There is more to the punch than just striking however. One important addition to your arsenal is learning how to 'miss' your attacker. By this I don't mean wildly swinging in the hope that you will hit something, but that by missing a target intentionally you can close the distance and, using parts of the arm and your shoulder, you can disrupt their balance.

As you can see from the image below, the defender has used the punch to close the distance, and their bodyweight and arm to aid in taking the attacker's balance. As you will see later on in the book, this is vital for performing sweeps and throws without having to rely on brute strength. This is especially important if you area fighting someone who is stronger or larger than yourself.

TYPES OF PUNCH

THE OBVERSE PUNCH AND JAB

The Obverse Punch and the Jab are both delivered from the same side as the lead foot. The way they differ is that the Obverse Punch is usually delivered with more force than the Jab (coming from the hip), whereas the Jab is delivered with a lot of speed and snap.

OBVERSE PUNCH

The Obverse Punch is often delivered in Walking Stance. This makes it an ideal punch to land from a stamping, kneeing or kicking motion. As your foot lands, plant the punch solidly into the target. Try to use your weight and forward momentum to punch into and through the target.

The Obverse Punch differs from the Jab because it does not rely on a snapping motion but is designed to hit into and through the target. It can be just as powerful as a Cross or Reverse Punch but utilises body weight far more.

Defender throws a Front Kick against an incoming attacker

As the defender lands they plant their lead foot and strike the attacker. Note how the defender is leaning towards the attacker, giving the punch much greater penetration

Defender chambers the punch by the hip

9

The traditional Obverse Punch is delivered from the hip rather than a high guard and is commonly used in a low Walking Stance, often starting out as the rear fist and being delivered whilst moving towards the attacker.

Defender moves towards the attacker using the current lead hand to 'spot' the target

Defender lands in Walking Stance and punches into the attacker just after landing their lead leg. A kihap is usually given at the same time as in this example

The area used to strike the target is the same as the Jab.

JAB

The Jab is best delivered with the lead leg posted (that is, planted), but can be delivered from the back foot (as a snap counter-punch). The Jab relies on speed rather than power with the hand leaving from and returning to the guard as quickly as possible.

The first picture shows the Jab delivered with the foot posted. It can be delivered from the position shown in the picture, but another way to do this is to step towards and slightly off to the side of the attacker and deliver the punch just after planting the foot.

The area used to strike the target is the entire front of the fist, with an emphasis placed on hitting with the first two knuckles. The reason for this is that as the kinetic power of the blow is focused onto a smaller area it increases the power of the strike.

PLANTED JAB

The Planted Jab is one of the most common punches in the world. It is quite simply a lead hand punch that is flicked out and back very quickly. Used to work through someone's guard or to set them up for a more devastating follow-up, the Jab can quickly wear an attacker down and even knock them out due to a cumulative effect.

Weight distribution should be 50–50. If you want to add a bit of 'sting' to your punch, lean in towards the attacker as you do so.

Further power can be added if you are using the Jab to close the distance in order to deliver a follow-up such as a Cross. In this case, step to the outside of the attacker and deliver the punch as you land, following this with a rear hand attack as soon as the Jab has landed. Weight distribution in this punch will be something more resembling 60–40 (with most of the weight being on your lead leg).

REAR LEG JAB

The second picture shows how the Jab can be delivered from the rear foot; note how the weight is on the back leg. At the same time the heel of the lead foot can be lifted. With this punch the weight is on the back foot. The drawback to this punch is that rather than landing into the punch and increasing the power by adding a proportion of your body weight, your body weight is actually moving away from the target.

This means that the punch is best delivered when you have been put onto your back foot by an incoming attacker and are able to use *their* body weight (as they come towards you) against themselves.

THE REVERSE AND CROSS

The Reverse and Cross Punches are a lot more powerful than the Obverse and Jab Punches. One core reason for this is that you can add a lot more body weight and Hip Twist by sinking into the punch (and raising your rear heel) and using the hips to drive through.

If you look at the pictures below you can see the difference between a traditional Reverse Punch and an enhanced Reverse/Cross Punch. As you can see, the Cross is delivered from a higher and shorter stance than the Reverse Punch.

As with the Obverse and Reverse Punches, the area used to strike the target is the entire front of the fist with an emphasis on the first two knuckles.

Traditional Reverse Punch – Note how the stance is evenly balanced with a 50–50 weight distribution between the lead and rear legs. The rear leg is also nearly dead straight (always avoid locking your limbs to prevent knee damage).

Enhanced Reverse Punch with bent leg – Note how the stance is as evenly balanced as the traditional stance. However the back leg has enabled the puncher to add their body weight (or a proportion of it) to the power of the strike.

THE CROSS

The Cross is the western equivalent of the Reverse Punch. As you can see, however, there are a number of fundamental differences between the two.

The most obvious difference is that the Cross is delivered from a high guard rather than from the hip. The stance that the defender assumes is also much higher, with the feet closer together and both legs slightly bent.

THE UPPERCUT AND SHOVEL HOOK

The Uppercut and Shovel Hook are two very powerful punches that can be devastating when delivered correctly. You may well be wondering how the Uppercut and Shovel Hook can be considered to be valid techniques when looking at the patterns in this book.

If you look at the Rising Block (found in Taegeuk Il Jang, but not in Saju Jirugi, nor Chon-Ji) the path that it follows can be easily adapted in order to provide you with the two extra punches. Taking the block and turning it into a punch like this does not change the nature of the pattern, nor indeed does it mean that the blocks are not blocks, it is just another way of looking at a certain move in the pattern and seeing how it can be applied.

THE SHOVEL HOOK

The Shovel Hook can be delivered in a number of ways and is especially effective once again if delivered with Hip Twist. The Shovel Hook differs from the basic Hook because it follows a diagonal upward path, rather than following a horizontal path. The best area to target with this punch is shown in the picture below.

It is best to use this punch to follow through on the tail of another punch. This is because it enables you to utilise the Hip Twist more effectively. One example of a combination that would allow this is a Cross followed by a Shovel Hook. This is because it allows you to drive your rear hip forward with the Cross and then drive the lead hip forward whilst you deliver the Hook. Couple this with lifting up on your toes and you will find that you are able to add a lot of power to the technique.

The area used to strike the target is the entire front of the fist.

THE UPPERCUT

The Uppercut is delivered from the knees, using the legs to drive the body upwards whilst the Hip Twist is used to add further power to the technique. At the same time as the knees are bent the punching hand is dropped back, down and with the hips moving back. As the legs are straightened, the punch is driven up and the hips twisted forward.

The area used to strike the target is the entire front of the fist.

THE OUTWARD HAMMER FIST

This strike is excellent for beginners and can be taught to a high degree of proficiency to a complete beginner in under five minutes. Obviously power can be increased through training for a longer period of time, but the essence of the strike, that is, the delivery and accuracy are already instinctive. Indeed, if you ever look at children and the way that they strike, another version of the Hammer Fist, the downward Hammer Fist is one of the most common strikes you will see them use.

As with the Low Block the Hammer Fist can follow a downward diagonal path but can also follow an outward horizontal path to the front, outward horizontal path to the rear and vertical downward path as demonstrated in the photos below.

The area used to strike the target is the fleshy underside of the fist, as shown in the pictures below.

THE PALM HEEL

There is a saying that you can often find: 'a push is a grab is a punch'. By this the person is referring to the motion of a push, a grab and a punch. Until the attack is delivered all three are identical, it is only when they land that you know whether the person is trying to push you, grab you or punch you. This can have you at a disadvantage, but it also allows you to invest less time in devising defences against them. As the push, grab or punch can all follow the same forward horizontal path, you do not need to work on three

different parries or blocks (although feel free if you want to). Obviously you will need to have slightly different defences for when the attacks actually land.

Similarly the fact that they are so similar also allows you to use one instead of another. This greatly opens up the number of applications you can find within the patterns and also allows you to not be bound to a certain technique if the situation does not demand it.

One example of this would be using a push, slap or Palm Heel instead of a punch when facing a weaker or younger attacker. This is because 'hitting' someone is deemed to be inappropriate for this type of attacker.

THE MODIFIED SLAP

Jim Wagner of Reality Based Personal Protection uses what he calls the 'modified slap'. This is a very important technique to use when dealing with someone who is much weaker than you and who does not warrant a full-blown strike to the head.

The action of the slap remains unchanged up to the point of impact. At that point, however, pull the blow down and away rather than through. Think of it as a 'glancing' blow.

When someone describes 'hitting' another person, the person that they are speaking to will generally assume that the 'hit' was made with a closed fist. It is therefore important that if you slap someone, you describe it as a slap when asked what actions you took and why you 'hit' someone in a self-defence situation.

The Palm Heel is delivered just as if you were attempting to push someone and can actually be used to push them as you strike them. The area used to strike the attacker is the base of the palm.

The Palm Heel is one of the most versatile strikes in your arsenal as every punch (not strike) can be open-handed rather than closed, giving you a much more socially acceptable solution.

THE ELBOW

The Elbow is a close-in technique that should only be used when you are too close to effectively deliver punches. Popularised by televised Muay Thai Fighters and films such as *Ong Bak*, the Elbow has caught the public's imagination.

Using one of the strongest bones in the arm along with a small striking area the Elbow can be a devastating technique to use. Aside from concussive damage, the Elbow is also good for causing cuts on an attacker's face, usually around the eyebrows and cheek bones.

Despite being a very simple technique to use, many styles treat it as an advanced technique and this is the same with taekwondo. The Elbow does not make an appearance in the patterns until much later and is then only taught as a Rising Elbow.

The easiest way to deliver an Elbow is on the horizontal plane, using an area near the tip of the elbow to strike the target.

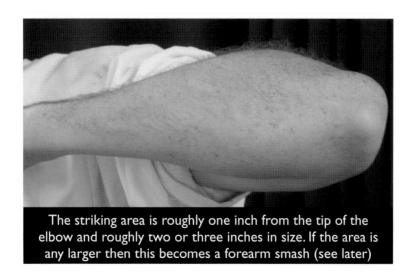

The striking area is roughly one inch from the tip of the elbow and roughly two or three inches in size. If the area is any larger then this becomes a forearm smash (see later)

THE LEAD ELBOW

As with lead punches, the Lead Elbow does not have as much power as its rear counterpart. It is a good weapon to use however, as it can be delivered rapidly in succession, using multiple strikes to maximise its effectiveness.

The defender has their guard up, but the attacker is too close to strike with a conventional punch

The defender drops their lead hand so that it is horizontal and palm down

The defender then folds their arm inwards whilst turning their upper body and lead leg towards and through the attacker. The defender ends the technique with their fist touching their chest, and their upper body torqued away from the attacker. They are now in the perfect position to follow this up with a combination such as Lead Outer Forearm Strike and Rear Hook.

THE REAR ELBOW

Delivered correctly, the Rear Elbow can be a real fight stopper. As with the Lead Elbow, the defender has deemed the attacker to be too close to strike them with a conventional strike.

The defender has their guard up, but the attacker is too close to strike with a conventional punch

The defender drops their rear hand so that it is horizontal and palm down

The defender then folds their arm inwards whilst turning their upper body towards and through the attacker. Simultaneously the weight is dropped and the rear leg slightly bent with the defender moving into a modified Walking Stance.

The defender ends the technique with their fist touching their chest, and their upper body torqued away from the attacker. They are now in the perfect position to follow this up with a combination such as Rear Forearm Strike, lead Shovel Hook. Note how the rear heel is raised, with the rear knee pointing more towards the lead leg rather than directly forward

SHOULDER STRIKING

Every schoolboy will have felt the effect of a Shoulder Strike at some point, usually as the school bully walks past them in the opposite direction and deliberately pushes their shoulder forward in to their victim's.

Done effectively the Shoulder Strike can knock your attacker off-balance and even cause damage, especially if the strike is against their face.

The rear shoulder is the most effective as it allows you to retract your shoulder before swinging it forward and in to the target. The strike can be delivered whilst walking normally or as part of the 'missing' punch, closing the gap. It is a very useful tool for taking the attacker's balance in order to set them up for a throw or reaping technique. This is demonstrated below.

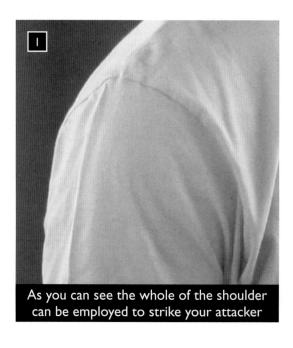

As you can see the whole of the shoulder can be employed to strike your attacker

9

LOOKING PAST THE 'PUNCH'

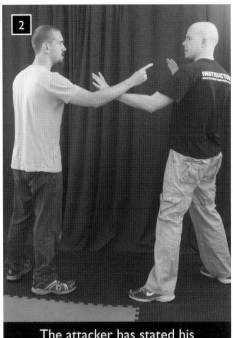

The attacker has stated his intent to do harm and is acting very aggressively

The defender knocks aside the attacker's arm whilst shooting forward with a punch

Deliberately aiming the punch past the attacker's head the defender strikes into the attacker's face with their shoulder, whilst pulling on the trapped arm

With little further effort the defender can now take the attacker to the floor

PULLING THE ATTACKER IN
(THE CHAMBER AS A WEAPON)

There are two reasons given as to why we chamber our fist at the hip when punching with the other hand. The first and most ridiculous is that it's an Elbow attack on someone to the rear. As you can see from the image, if we apply this in the traditional sense it doesn't work. It's also just as unworkable in a street situation.

Student in Walking Stance, trying to do a
Rear Elbow to an attacker to their rear

The other reason put forward is that the withdrawing of the hand gives power to the one punching and improves hip-twist and therefore gives yet more power. This is closer but still isn't quite 'right'. I say 'right' because I'm not going to say that something is right or wrong. I might say it's ridiculous because that's my opinion, but what's 'right' or 'wrong' isn't for me to say.

It is better to look at the retraction as a combination of two things. The first is covered in the above paragraph. The second factor is that when the defender retracts their hand as far and low as their hip they are actually pulling the attacker in towards them. This is how the power for the outgoing punch is both increased and generated.

As the defender yanks back and down they are aiming to do a number of things:

- cause a whipping action in the neck of their opponent which in turn disorientates them

- disrupt their opponent's height, width and depth, therefore taking their balance

- generate power for their punch by having the attacker literally walk into the technique

- prevent the attacker from striking the defender through doing all of the above.

As you can see from the image when I yank the attacker forward and down their head turns and the rear hand flies out. The attacker takes a step forward and bends at the hip. They are now in a low, elongated and unbalanced stance whereas I have retained my upright and balanced position. Rather than having to stretch into order to strike through the attacker, I can use their momentum to aid me in doing so. Hopefully their lead foot will step closer to me aiding me in any follow-up sweep or throw that I might enter into. This is where the Chunbi Sweep comes in handy.

The defender grabs the attacker's arm securing a strong hold

The defender then yanks their arm sharply back and down towards their hip

3

This causes the attacker to step forward, lean downwards and their head to turn to the side.

At the same time as they pull back to their hip, the defender strikes out with a punch, increasing the power and penetration of the strike

At all times the defender has retained control of the attacker's arm and kept this control even whilst punching the attacker, and taking the attacker to the ground. This gives the defender an excellent opportunity to either injure the limb in order to help them in escaping or to use it in order to control the attacker (if they were a police officer or door supervisor for example).

The good thing about the retraction is that it can be done even if they have grabbed you by the arm or wrist. Simply do a Centre Lock using Lower Outer Forearm and pull.

Practice this carefully as the force generated by the pull can be quite surprising and accidental knockouts are more than possible.

10

LOOKING PAST THE WALKING STANCE

Although L-Stance was covered earlier on in the book, this volume will not look at applications that can be used. The reason for this is because it is only used four times in Chon-Ji with every other stance being Walking Stance. As a result, applications for this stance will be covered in later volumes in which it makes a higher number of appearances.

Looking at Walking Stance as it is currently taught there is very little you would use it for outside of the dojang. Taekwondo competitors are hardly going to drop into Walking Stance whilst sparring because it's not the best stance to be in when kicking. Karateka do so because they rely on Reverse Punch as their main scoring tool.

When on the street facing a somewhat belligerent yobbo, going into Walking Stance is not only going to show him that you know too much for your own good (and therefore make dealing with him much harder) but it's going to severely limit your options when it comes to moving into or away from him. It's also highly unstable if attacked from the side.

So what on earth is the point of this stance? Why would, or how could, you use it in a practical manner?

The most obvious use is against someone pushing you backwards whilst they are moving forwards (rather than just pushing in more of a striking manner). This is one of the most common techniques taught when people ask 'yes ... but why?'

Setting yourself into a modified Walking Stance means that you can set your weight to resist the push and try to counter-attack.

We shall now look at less obvious and more effective uses. There are a number of ways that you can move into Walking Stance. The Step Method, where you move straight forward and into the stance, is more suited to kicking applications.

The attacker is pushing with both hands and the defender has set themselves into Walking Stance

The more interesting applications come when you are already in Walking Stance and either moving forward or backward. It must be borne in mind that on the whole this is a transitionary stance. You should move into and out of the stance as quickly as you would any other more dynamic stance; it's purely because of the way it's taught that students think it's 'rooted'.

Turning to the left or right involves a slightly different shape to the movement. With the Crescent method, the lead foot comes back to the rear foot and then back out so that it becomes the rear foot, completing the movement.

Breaking it down this means that there are six movements for Walking Stance:

1. moving forwards whilst in a non-Walking Stance position
2. moving backwards whilst in a non-Walking Stance position
3. moving forwards whilst in Walking Stance
4. moving backwards whilst in Walking Stance
5. turning to the left or right whilst in Walking Stance

Attacker and defender facing
each other

The most simple application for this is a straightforward stamping Front Kick to the inside or outside of either the lead or rear leg of the attacker. Both attacks can be used to hurt or, if the situation is more serious, injure the attacker by not only hitting pressure points but also destroying their kneecap.

Defender steps forward and to the
outside of the attacker

As the defender lands their foot
they stamp and rake down the
outside of the attacker's leg

10

LOOKING PAST THE WALKING STANCE

SHORT ANALYSIS

Whichever leg you target, the attack is going to cause the attacker to buckle, bringing their head down and forward. Balance will be disrupted and their arms may well come forward.

If the rear leg is attacked it will either buckle, or be pushed further back (depending on the actual attack) the latter causing the attacker to put either one or both hands onto the floor for support.

MOVING BACKWARDS WHILST IN A
NON-WALKING STANCE POSITION

This is good for when someone is trying to grab you from behind and prior to them lifting you. Shunt your leg straight back and between their legs aiming to actually strike one of them. If you can, butt your bottom back and into their groin whilst moving your head backwards

The attacker has grabbed the defender around the waist pinning their arms

In order to make lifting as difficult as possible the defender shoves their rear backwards into the groin of the attacker

3

As soon as they have done the rear attack the defender whips their head back, attempting to hit the attacker

4

As soon as then have done this the defender shunts their leg backwards into the attacker's leg

SHORT ANALYSIS

If done with sufficient force, this will cause the attacked leg to either lock out or shunt backwards as well as causing the attacker to bring their head forward and down. The bottom strike into the groin will shock and hurt the attacker, causing them to loosen their grip and bring their head forward and down. The rear headbutt will cause the attacker to move their head back and away (regardless as to whether you actually strike with it). Striking the face will cause them to loosen their grip and move their hands to the affected area.

MOVING FORWARDS WHILST IN WALKING STANCE

Move the leg forwards ensuring that you trace the crescent with your foot and hook behind their foot, lean your knee forward as you sink down and lock out their knee.

The defender slides their right foot forward and around the attacker's right foot

Note how the knees are now touching; it is vital that the defender move quickly to avoid being locked themselves

The defender now leans their weight forward, bending their lead leg. The attacker's leg is forced backward until it is locked out

Steady, constant forward pressure allows the defender to take the attacker to the ground

SHORT ANALYSIS

The attacker's leg will lock straight out. Their rear leg will step back in order to lessen the pressure on the knee and their arms may well go back with the head coming down and forward. If sufficient speed and force is applied at the start of the technique their knee joint will be damaged.

MOVING BACKWARDS WHILST IN WALKING STANCE

The attacker's leg is locked and their toes are pointing in the direction in which the defender will be moving their leg

This actually makes a good follow-up from the above technique. The defender has already destroyed the attacker's height, width and balance and the defender's lead leg is nicely placed behind the attacker's lead leg. Because of all the above factors this technique requires very little strength and just relies on good technique.

With a sharp movement, the defender moves their lead foot back towards their rear foot

Continuing the motion the defender moves into Walking Stance, taking the attacker to the ground or severely stretching them out

The application is made all the more effective because the defender's foot is moving in the direction that the attacker's toes are pointing. This is a key factor in sweeping.

At the very least this will cause the attacker to go into a highly extended stance, put one or both hands on the floor and leave them unable to do any form of offensive move. The ideal response is that the attacker is swept completely to the floor whilst damaging their leg and groin muscles.

MOVING TO THE LEFT OR RIGHT WHILST IN WALKING STANCE

This movement is again good for taking the attacker down. You can use the crescent motion to get behind the attacker's foot, the 'punch' to destroy their balance (see 'Looking Past the Punch') and the chamber for Low Block to get a good grip. Because their balance is completely destroyed by the 'punch', good technique means that this is not a matter of who's strongest being able to perform the reap. This technique has been tested in research with male versus female and short versus tall using decreasing amounts of compliancy and so long as the criteria are met, this technique works perfectly.

The defender has taken the attacker's balance whilst stepping forward into right Walking Stance

10

LOOKING PAST THE WALKING STANCE

10

The defender secures a good grip with their left hand on the attacker's right arm

The defender then sharply slides their lead foot back towards their rear foot, whilst pulling down with their left hand

Turning to the left the defender continues the motion of their foot whilst continuing to pull down with their left.

The attacker is taken to the floor landing in front of the defender's lead foot with their arm locked up. The defender can now finish as necessary

Depending on the situation, the defender can enhance the downward movement by pushing down on the attacker's chest or head with the right hand. The latter move should only be used in dire situations as it allows you to drive the back of the head into the ground.

WALKING STANCE ON THE GROUND

Walking Stance is far more flexible than you might think and is a 'stance' commonly used in grappling whilst on the floor (as well as being good for throwing whilst standing up).

This was first really noticed during a Vadim Kolganov seminar on Sambo. One of the throws he performed was straight out of the ITF Pattern Do San. This warranted a closer look at what else he was using whilst tying Paul Carthy of Torbay BJJ (Brazilian Ju Jitsu) (the host) up in knots. The next technique that particularly stood out was the position his legs and arms were in when he was in the side mount and attempting to control Paul.

The image below shows traditional Walking Stance from the side. Note the position of the chambered fist, the lead knee and the lead hand. This is both a good strong stance and one which can stop an attacker dead.

Looking at the image below you can see the same stance but on the floor. The positioning is still the same but the emphasis of the balance and weight distribution has now been changed so that the right-hand side of my body is putting the weight down towards the floor.

10

Finally, if we add an attacker we can see how the arm performing the lower outer forearm is controlling the attacker's head, the hand chambered at the hip is controlling their right arm and my body is exerting pressure onto their chest. The latter means that not only do they find it difficult to move but also to breathe. If they try to shift position in order to escape I can exert more pressure onto their head and chest whilst using my feet to keep me in this dominant position.

From here the defender is able to finish them by attacking their eyes with either hand. No matter how hard they try to resist your fingers coming in, you can still overcome them and gouge their eyes. Of course this is a last resort technique and one that should only be used whilst finishing what is a potentially life threatening situation, with little or no injury to yourself whilst giving you every opportunity to get away..

The defender is able to attack the attacker's eyes despite the attacker attempting to resist

GET TRAINING

Although I have illustrated how similar Walking Stance can be when compared to a grappling position, it is vital that you don't assume that just because you know how to get into Walking Stance that you can automatically grapple. Indeed, this sort of grappling is often referred to as 'crappling', because it doesn't match the standard of established Grappling styles.

It is vital that you train with grapplers in Sambo, Judo, BJJ, Mixed Martial Arts (MMA), or Submission for example, as it is only through training with them that you will be able to understand the mechanics. It's also great fun!

Also, bear in mind that these techniques are shown with an attacker who is a non-Grappler in mind. Attempting these techniques against a trained Grappler (if indeed you're able to get into such a dominant position in the first place) will most likely end up in you being on the receiving end of some very nasty techniques.

KNEE KICK

As previously mentioned 'a push is a grab is a punch'. There is a new saying when it comes to Walking Stance. 'A step is a knee is a stamp is a kick.'

The Knee Kick is an especially powerful, short range technique that requires very little skill to deliver powerfully.

The defender grabs hold of their attacker by either the neck or the shoulders

The defender should not link their fingers. Note how the hands are placed and gripped

The defender skips the kicking leg back to the rear

The defender then pulls the attacker sharply forward and drives the knee forward and up into the attacker's chest.

Note how the defender has used the attacker to retain their balance whilst trying to drive their knee through the attacker

To finish, the defender turns sharply and throws the attacker to the floor

FRONT SNAP KICK

The Front Snap Kick is another technique that is close to an instinctive move. Everyone can do a kick, it may come straight up and out, or may look more like a football (soccer) kick, but it is still a Front Kick.

The Front Snap Kick is so-called because it is delivered using a short, sharp strike. Due to this, the Front Snap Kick can be used at a shorter range than the Front Kick. The kick can, with very little modification, be used to 'jam' an incoming attacker.

Attacker and defender are facing off at a distance slightly greater than that of punching range

2

As the attacker starts to move in, the defender drives out a Low Section Front Snap Kick. The kick stops the attacker in their tracks as it strikes their knee.

Note how the leg is still bent whilst striking. The aim is not to penetrate but to strike quickly and retract

3

Once the kicking leg has landed, the defender moves in with follow-up techniques

STAMPING KICK

The Stamping Kick is a close-range technique that can be used to take the initiative from the attacker.

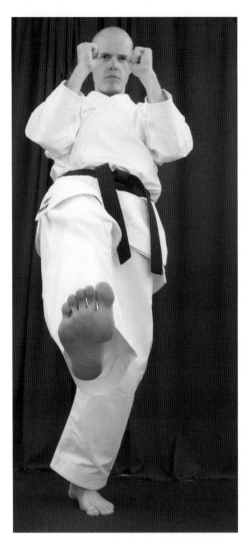

From a high guard position the defender brings their rear knee forward and up high

The Stamp Kick comes down onto the attacker's kneecap or inside thigh.

The defender lands into the attacker. In a real confrontation the technique would be pushed through the target with the aim being to break the attacker's knee

LOOKING PAST THE WALKING STANCE

It is common amongst 'karate' styles of martial arts to block kicks to the middle or low section with the arms. As any experienced kickboxer can attest, this can leave the defender's head wide open to follow-up hand strikes. It also leaves them in a disadvantaged position for follow-up attacks of their own.

One way to avoid having to drop the guard whilst defending against kicks is to use the legs.

1

The attacker comes towards the defender with a 'yobbo' or 'soccer' kick. This is different from the typical martial arts kick because it comes in at an angle, but is more likely to be encountered on the street if kicks are being thrown

2

The defender raises their lead leg and points their shin slightly outward, stopping the attack with the outside of their shin. Note, it is possible to block with the shin directly, but unless you are conditioning yourself to do this, that is, by practicing Muay Thai, it's really not worth the pain that this can cause

10

LOOKING PAST THE WALKING STANCE

3

As soon as contact is made (or even before), the defender kicks their leg out, pushing the attacker's leg out and away from themselves. This completely changes the direction of the attacker's momentum

4

The defender places their leg back down into a balanced stance and counter-attack, whilst the attacker is forced off-course and lands off-balance

11

SAJU JIRUGI – HOW TO PERFORM IT

Start in Neutral Stance

Step forward with right leg into Walking Stance, Obverse Punch

Turn left into Walking Stance and perform left Low Block

Step forward into right Walking Stance with right Obverse Punch

Turn left into Walking Stance and perform left Low Block

Step forward with right Obverse Punch

Turn left into Walking Stance and perform left Low Block

Step forward with right Obverse Punch

Come back to
the centre and into
neutral stance

Step forward with left
leg into Walking Stance,
Obverse Punch

Turn right into Walking
Stance and perform
right Low Block

Step forward with left Obverse Punch

Turn right into Walking Stance and perform right Low Block

Step forward with left Obverse Punch

Turn right into Walking Stance and perform right Low Block

Step forward with left Obverse Punch

Come back to the centre and into Neutral Stance

12

CHON-JI – HOW TO PERFORM IT

Start in Neutral Stance

Turn 90° left into left
Walking Stance, Low Block

Step forward into
right Walking Stance,
Obverse Punch

Turn 180° right into
right Walking Stance,
Low Block

Step forward into left Walking Stance,
Obverse Punch

Turn 90° left into
left Walking Stance,
Low Block

Step forward into right Walking Stance, Obverse Punch

Turn 180° right into right Walking Stance, Low Block

Step forward into left Walking Stance, Obverse Punch

Left 90° turn into right L-Stance, left Inner Forearm Block

Step forward into right Walking Stance, right Obverse Punch

CHON-JI – HOW TO PERFORM IT

Turn 180° right into
left L-Stance, right Inner
Forearm Block

Step forward into left Walking
Stance, Obverse Punch

Turn 90° left into right
L-Stance, left Inner
Forearm Block

Step forward into
right Walking Stance,
Obverse Punch

Turn 180° right turn
into left L-Stance, right
Inner Forearm Block

Step forward into
Left Walking Stance,
Obverse Punch

Step forward into
right Walking Stance,
Obverse Punch

Step backward into
left Walking Stance,
Obverse Punch

Step backward into right Walking
Stance, Obverse Punch

Come back to the
centre and into
Neutral Stance

13

SAJU JIRUGI AND CHON-JI APPLICATIONS

Although previous chapters have dealt with techniques from all of the patterns, we shall now look at specific applications for Saju Jirugi and Chon-Ji. Because of the similarity of the two patterns there is a lot of cross-over in the applications.

It is key to remember that although you might well be facing a trained martial artist, the likelihood is that you will be facing someone with little or no martial arts training and that therefore they may well lack the focus, control or power you can expect from trained martial artists. This is all to your advantage as long as you bear in mind that you may well be facing a martial artist and respond with all the focus, control and power you can muster.

APPLICATION 1 – ALSO FOUND IN CHON JI – PRE-EMPTIVE

The defender steps forward as if they are about to right punch the attacker but instead 'punch' to the left-hand side of the attacker's head. The defender's right leg should go behind the attacker's right leg. Note how the feet are positioned

The defender reaches up with their left hand as they would were they performing the technique 'properly' but instead grasp the attacker's upper forearm/shoulder (clothing or flesh does not really matter). The defender turns 90° to the left, whilst simultaneously pulling their left hand down into the block and shooting their right leg back and out as they would in the pattern using the crescent method. This takes the attacker to the ground

The defender moves their right leg forward (as if taking the next step) and drops down onto their ribs, punching as they do

SHORT ANALYSIS

This application takes and keeps the initiative. It is completely pre-emptive and does not rely on the attacker doing a specific technique.

The step forward coupled with the missing punch takes the attacker's balance whilst causing them pain. Because of the penetration of the step and the punch, the attacker's centre of balance is moved at least a foot back behind them. This means that once the turn begins, it does not require strength to take them to the ground, but relies on speed and a good crescent method of stepping for the Walking Stance.

Performed correctly this technique leaves the attacker on the floor stunned and in pain, giving the defender ample opportunity to make their escape.

13

SAJU JIRUGI AND CHON-JI APPLICATIONS

APPLICATION 2 – ALSO FOUND IN CHON JI – PRE-EMPTIVE

1 The defender steps forward as if they are about to punch their attacker but instead 'punch' to the left-hand side of the attacker's head. Their right leg should go behind the attacker's right leg (see *Technique 1*).

The defender places the knobbly bit (see inset) of their wrist around St.9, LI.18, and LI. 17 (see Appendix: Pressure Points) on the left-hand side of the attacker's neck

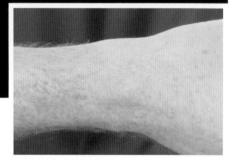

2 The defender reaches up with their left hand as the defender would were the defender performing the technique properly but instead places their forearm on the right-hand side of the attacker's neck and simultaneously pulls their right hand towards themselves whilst pushing their forearm away. This will cause a pincer movement to the neck and should be performed slowly during training

3

The defender moves their right leg back and maintains the pressure on the neck as they turn 90° to the left. This will again cause the attacker to go to the floor.

Note: It is important that the right leg be placed behind the attacker's right leg as this prevents them from turning out of the technique and allows the defender to use their leg as a fulcrum for taking the attacker down

SHORT ANALYSIS

This is another pre-emptive application that closes the distance between the defender and the attacker and which works well with adrenaline through using simple smashing (the Elbow) and clubbing (the forearm) strikes. Either of the strikes can be enough in themselves to finish the fight.

The turn does not require much skill and again relies more on speed. Although the turn is performed better if both people are the same height, the strikes and pincer can still be performed by shorter people on taller people, especially if they use other attacks to lower them.

Performed quickly and with sufficient pressure the attacker can often be rendered unconscious in the initial stages of the technique. This is because the 'pincer' movement turns into a double strike.

SAJU JIRUGI AND CHON-JI APPLICATIONS

APPLICATION 3 – ALSO FOUND IN CHON-JI - DEFENCE AGAINST A RIGHT FRONT KICK

The attacker comes in with a right Front Kick. Note that this is not a Traditional Front Kick, but a yobbo/soccer kick as found on the street. As such it comes from a slightly different angle and rises

The defender steps out to 4 or 5 o'clock and jams the kick keeping their hands up in high guard

The jam should cause the attacker to land unbalanced and open, with the defender on the inside

The defender performs a low Front Snap Kick in to the inside of thigh or knee points, landing forward rather than retracting

As the defender lands they strike out with either a right punch or Elbow, continuing with any follow-ups they feel are necessary

Note how the defender could easily Chunbi Sweep and extend the attacker's stance to the extent that it damages the groin and takes them to the floor

SHORT ANALYSIS

Although this application relies on the attacker carrying out a kick and therefore having the initiative from the start, it also starts at a greater distance. Often with such attacks there are a number of clear steps as the attacker gears up for the kick. This means that although the attacker has the initiative, the defender has time to set themselves for what is coming.

The jam, for anyone who has not experienced it, is incredibly painful, especially when it is not anticipated. The way that it is rolled out ensures that the attacker will land in an open and unbalanced stance, completely off-target and unable to follow up with further attacks without having to reset.

The follow-up strikes by the defender inflict more pain and take the attacker further off-balance, giving the defender a good opportunity to make their escape.

APPLICATION 4 – AGAINST RIGHT CROSS-HAND GRAB (VARIATION 1) – ALSO FOUND IN CHON-JI

The attacker has grabbed the defender's right hand

The defender performs a Centre Lock, taking the attacker off-balance and down to the ground

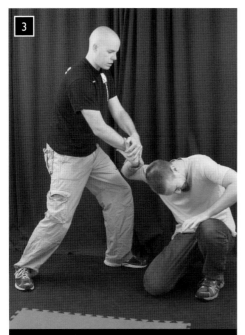

Retaining control of the attacker's hand, the defender performs a right punch, using the attacker's hand to assist in the strike

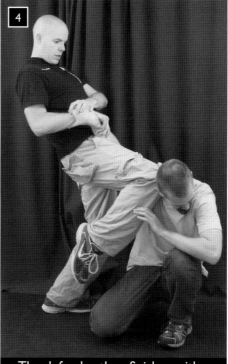

The defender then finishes with a right knee to the face

SHORT ANALYSIS

The Centre Lock is a devastating technique as it requires very little pressure to badly injure an attacker's wrist. The technique not only causes intense pain and discomfort, but also disrupts the attacker's balance. Often the attacker will be forced to their knees in an often futile attempt to alleviate the pain. The knee to the face is, therefore, easy to perform, especially after the right punch has stunned the attacker.

There are many ways that someone can be grabbed by the wrist, but these are usually rare as attacks. A grab to the wrist should be considered as a counter to an action that you have carried out. For example, a grab to the testicles will cause an attacker to flinch back and grab your wrist in order to remove it.

APPLICATION 5 – AGAINST DOUBLE LAPEL GRAB/NECK GRAB (VARIATION 2) – ALSO FOUND IN CHON-JI

The defender shrugs their shoulders up, momentarily trapping the attacker's hands. At the same time the defender steps their right leg back slightly

The defender brushes the attacker's face with their fingers, leading their mind to defending against a high attack

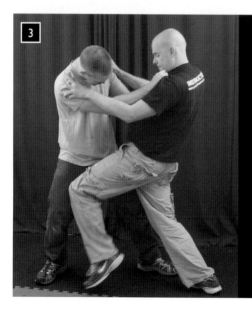

The defender then launches a lead Knee to the inside of the attacker's opposite knee/inside thigh. For available points see Appendix

4

The defender then launches forward with a rear knee strike into the same target area as before

5

The defender lands their right leg forward into a strong stance whilst delivering a right Elbow

6

The defender then sweeps their right leg out to the leg, either hyper-extending the attacker's groin, or taking them to the ground

SHORT ANALYSIS

The attacker is concentrating on one major thing, holding onto the defender (no matter how briefly) as well as on attacking. The brush to the face will force them to concentrate on the possibility of an attack to the High Section.

This won't be a conscious decision and will cause them to flinch back. The attack to the Low Section will therefore cause more shock and pain, whilst bringing their head back down. The inside of the thigh is highly sensitive compared to the outside due to the latter being bashed and brushed on a daily basis.

With a number of pressure points in the target area, the first knee will activate at least one, making it much more sensitive and receptive to further strikes. Therefore the much more powerful rear knee will have a far greater effect than if it had been delivered on its own.

Both knees will disrupt the attacker's balance, possibly ending the attack there and then. If not, the Elbow will be given greater power due to the defender landing forward and sinking their weight down into the strike.

The final sweep further disrupts the attacker's balance, giving the defender a good chance to leave the scene.

APPLICATION 6 – AGAINST A STANDING GRAPPLE – ALSO IN CHON-JI

1

The defender can be either square on or have their right leg back. The attacker has grabbed the defender in order for a standing grapple, the defender has grabbed the attacker with their left hand on the attacker's shoulder and their right hand on the attacker's collar

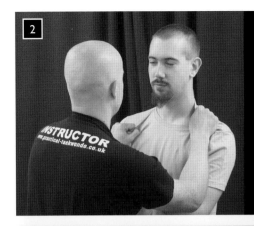

2

Note the position of the defender's hands

3

The defender rotates the thumb on their right hand and into the side of the attacker's neck, attacking the neck points there

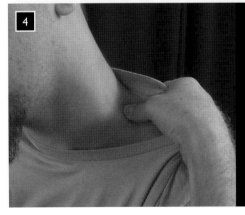

4

Note how the thumb is deep in the neck with the collar adding additional pressure

At the same time as number two, the defender pulls the attacker towards themselves with their left hand and 'punches' forward with their right. Note how this turns the attacker anti-clockwise

The defender brings their left Elbow up into a short, sharp strike to GB20 (see Appendix: Pressure Points).

The defender then extends their left arm back out, placing the forearm across the attacker's throat

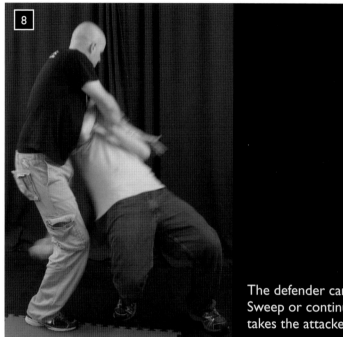

The defender can now either Chunbi Sweep or continue the motion and takes the attacker to the ground

SHORT ANALYSIS

Obviously this is a re-active technique as shown, however there is no reason that the defender cannot seize the attacker and perform this technique.

The neck points can be especially tender; however the pressure exerted by the thumb into the neck is still a good tool if this doesn't prove to be the case. Either way this should be viewed as a supplementary technique and all effort should be put into the push and pull.

The Elbow strike to the back of the head is a good stunning technique. By 'stunning', 'distracting' is also meant.

Turning the attacker around leaves them at a severe disadvantage and prevents them from performing any follow-up attacks whilst attempting to regain their balance and turn around.

Rather than sweep, the defender can also simply step sharply back and pull the attacker down that way.

APPLICATION 7 – AGAINST TWIN LAPEL GRAB/SHOULDER GRAB FOR KNEE

This defence is for when the defender is facing someone who is going to knee the defender. Generally if the attacker is going to do such an attack it will be with the right leg and they will need to extend it back (or even switch stance), in order to get as much power as possible into the attack. This should give some warning of their intent.

At the same time as number two, the defender pulls the attacker towards themselves with their left hand and 'punches' forward with their right. Note how this turns the attacker anti-clockwise

The defender then steps their right leg back

As the attacker attempts to knee, the defender double palms to the inside of their thigh, aiming for just above the knee

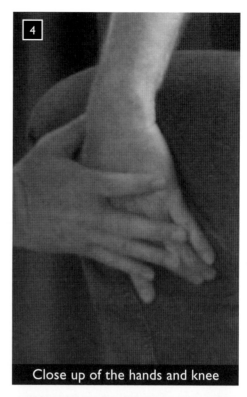

Close up of the hands and knee

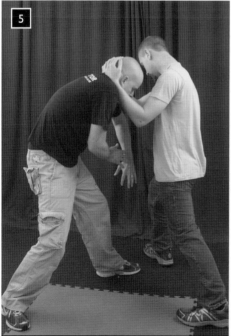

This will cause the attacker to land in a more unbalanced and open stance

Staying low, the attacker then uses a right Shovel Hook into the kidneys or floating rib

SAJU JIRUGI AND CHON-JI APPLICATIONS

The defender then throws a right roundhouse knee into the attacker's rear leg, landing the leg behind the attacker's

The defender quickly rises up and performs a Chunbi Sweep after putting their right hand across the attacker's face

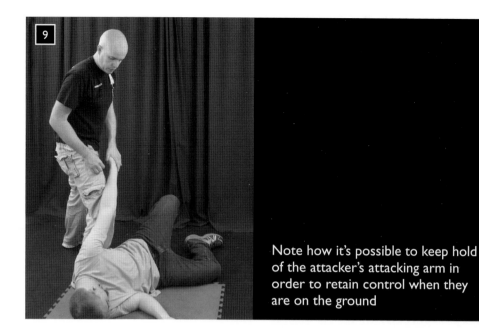

9

Note how it's possible to keep hold of the attacker's attacking arm in order to retain control when they are on the ground

SHORT ANALYSIS

A knee to the face is something best avoided, in fact a knee to any location of the body is best avoided.

It was found that smothering Knee Kicks is possible, however this only smothers the knee and does not prevent the attacker from delivering more knees. Further experimentation found that creating distance coupled with the parry and block to the inside of the knee allowed the defender to counter-attack.

Initially all of the defender's responses are concentrated on the attacker's Low and Mid Section. The parry and block are directed to the point on the inside of the thigh just above the knee, and the motion should be carried out and past the defender's left side. This causes the attacker to lose their balance much more.

The punch to the Floating Ribs or Kidney is really more of a wind-up for the knee and it does not matter if it misses or is missed out entirely as the knee should take precedent.

Once the knee has landed successfully the attacker will not only be in a great deal of pain but their balance will also be totally disrupted, which is key in enabling the follow-up sweep to work effectively.

APPLICATION 8 – AGAINST TWIN LAPEL GRAB

The attacker has grabbed the defender by the clothing

The defender brings their left hand up in a strike to GB20 and/or grabs the attacker's hair

This shows the whole target area. The slap should start at the hairline and go up. Any lower and you will miss

At the same time they step their left leg forward. As the foot lands, the defender pulls sharply back and down to the left on the attacker's hair

13

SAJU JIRUGI AND CHON-JI APPLICATIONS

As soon as they have pulled the attacker's head back, they punch into the throat area

Letting go of the head the defender performs a Rear Knee to the attacker, using it to knock them away

SHORT ANALYSIS

There is nothing subtle in this technique whatsoever. It is short, sharp and to the point. The attacker is totally focused on holding onto the defender.

The slap to GB20 will come as a shock, and will make them feel as if they have been shocked.

Coupled with a hair grab and pull and the step forward, the punch to the throat will continue the backward motion of the attacker causing them to lose their balance, especially if the hair pull is sharp.

The knee allows the defender to help the attacker on their way backward and therefore helps in letting them escape the situation.

SAJU JIRUGI AND CHON-JI APPLICATIONS

APPLICATION 9 – ALSO FOUND IN CHON-JI. DEFENCE AGAINST SAME SIDE GRAB

The attacker grabs the defender's left hand with their right hand

The defender brings the left hand up into a Back Fist. Note how it turns and opens up the attacker's arm, bending their arm back towards their shoulder

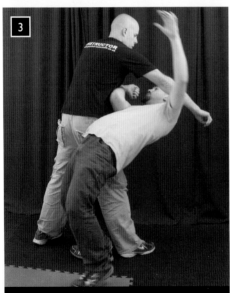

The defender steps forward as if to perform a right punch but does not strike, instead they hit the attacker with their shoulder

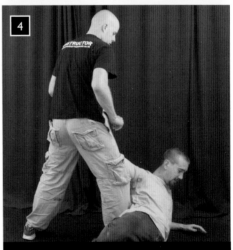

The force of the technique sends the attacker rapidly backwards, leaving the defender to follow-up with finishing techniques or to make their escape. In this case, the attacker was taken to the floor

This application is relatively non-offensive and can be used in situations that do not necessarily warrant a more percussive response.

The initial Back Fist will break the grip of the attacker or cause them to suffer a lot of discomfort if they continue to hold on. This will cause them to bend back and therefore lose a lot of their balance.

The shoulder barge can then be used to complete their loss of balance and give the defender enough space to make their escape should they need to.

This does not, however, end the attack and although it opens up the space between attacker and defender, it does mean that the defender might well have to face another attack from the attacker.

APPLICATION 10 – PRE-EMPTIVE HAIR GRAB THROW – ALSO FOUND IN SAJU JIRUGI

The attacker is 'bigging it up' so the defender moves forward and grabs the attacker's hair with their left hand and the attacker's jaw with the right hand

13

SAJU JIRUGI AND CHON-JI APPLICATIONS

At the same time the defender steps their right foot/leg round the attacker's lead leg to stop them stepping out of the technique

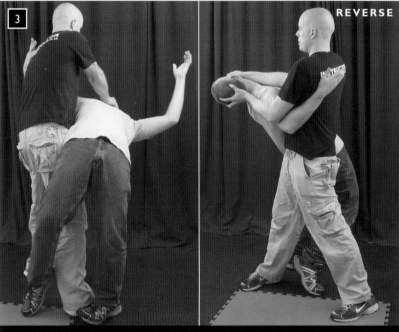

The defender then pulls on the hair and pushes with the right hand, twisting the attacker's head up and anti-clockwise, causing the body to turn in that direction.

13

SAJU JIRUGI AND CHON-JI APPLICATIONS

The defender then turns to the left and pulls sharply down with the left hand whilst performing Low Block

The attacker is left on the ground, with the defender finishing as necessary

SHORT ANALYSIS

This application is excellent in that it does not rely on the attacker to do anything other than state their willingness to cause injury and harm. Although best performed at short range, the distance can be closed if need be.

The application is very easy to perform and, due to the pressure being exerted on the back of the head and chin of the attacker, requires very little strength to make it work effectively.

APPLICATION 11 – AGAINST SAME SIDE GRAB (RIGHT) FACING ATTACKER

The defender hooks their left hand over the attacker's grabbing arm

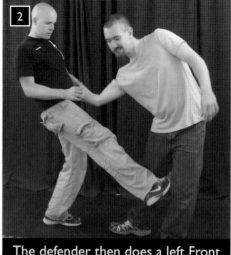

The defender then does a left Front Kick to the inside of the attacker's right thigh, just above the knee

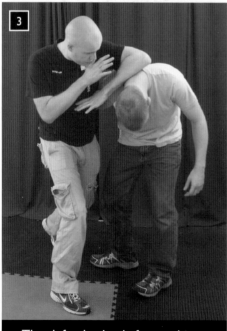

The defender lands forward into Walking Stance, performing a left Elbow to the right side of the attacker's head

The defender then performs a Rear Knee, whilst pulling down on the attacker's head

5

Keeping the attacker's head
down the defender lands and
performs a downward Elbow to
the back of the head

SHORT ANALYSIS

Because of the attacker holding onto the defender, the lead Front Kick is
made all the more viable as the attacker effectively aids the defender in
keeping their balance.

The defender's actions will cause a massive and rapid shock to the attacker
who is most likely expecting a completely different outcome and response.
The 'natural' response would be for the defender to try to pull their hand
away, however this application utilises the grab and sees the defender moving
forward into the attacker.

None of the techniques require a great deal of skill or finesse and work well
with adrenalin. This takes the fight to the attacker and keeps the initiative
firmly with the defender once commenced.

APPLICATION 12 – AGAINST LEFT SHOULDER GRAB (FROM SIDE) WITH LEFT HAND

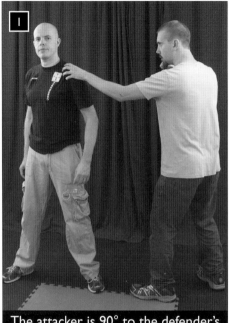

The attacker is 90° to the defender's left and has grabbed the left shoulder

The defender quickly reaches up and pins the grabbing hand with their right hand, pressing in on the web of the thumb

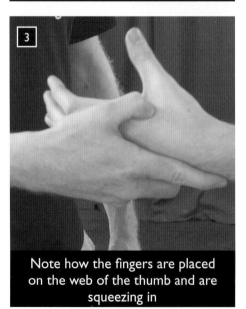

Note how the fingers are placed on the web of the thumb and are squeezing in

The defender turns towards the attacker using their left leg to attack the attacker's lead leg/knee (this is most likely to be their left leg)

5

Retaining control of the attacker's hand, the defender does a Low Block down, into and through their back, aiming for the bottom of their ribs

6

The defender then performs rear knee to GB31 at mid-thigh

7

The defender lands and performs a Chunbi Sweep

SHORT ANALYSIS

This application again requires little in the areas of skill or finesse. Aside from the grab (which could be to any part of the attacker's hand or arm), all the other responses by the defender are clubbing or kneeing-type strikes.

The application does not require fancy footwork from the defender as once they have turned the only direction they take is forward into and through the attacker. It also enables them to stay on the outside of the attacker, closing down their options for attack.

APPLICATION 13 – AGAINST LEFT SHOULDER GRAB (FROM SIDE) WITH RIGHT HAND

The attacker is 90° to the defender's left and has grabbed the left

The defender quickly reaches up and pins the grabbing hand with their right hand, pressing in on the web of the thumb. See previous technique

The defender turns towards the attacker using their left leg to attack the attacker's lead leg/knee (this is most likely to be their right leg)

Turn 90° to the left and perform Low Block into the attacker's groin

The defender 'punches' by grabbing the attacker's head

and pulls it down onto a right knee

SHORT ANALYSIS

Because this is a variation of Application 14, there is little to add. It should be noted however that the strike to the groin will cause the attacker to fold forward (no matter how much) and therefore will aid the defender in their knee attack.

APPLICATION 14 – AGAINST A LAPEL GRAB – SAJU JIRUGI CHON-JI

The attacker has grabbed the defender by the lapel

The defender quickly slaps the attacker across the face with their right hand

Continuing the blow the defender places their right hand over the attacker's hand

The defender then twists their right hand clockwise keeping it tight into their chest and, using both hands, quickly snaps their hands forward whilst sinking their weight

SHORT ANALYSIS

This application does rely on the attacker grabbing the defender. However this grab aids the defender, especially if the attacker has an especially strong grip and has entwined their fist in the defender's clothing.

Barring the slap, all of the application uses what could be viewed as a natural response from the defender. When grabbed in such a way, it is natural for people to try to pry the offending hand from their clothes.

Although the prying is expected, the follow-up is not. The rotation of the wrist coupled with the snap forward has the potential to break the wrist very quickly. At the same time the attacker will be brought down and forward as the defender steps back and down themselves. Whereas the attacker will need to place their free hand on the floor for balance, the defender is free to quickly rise and finish as they require.

Done with sufficient force and intent, this technique requires little skill and can be devastating. The way that the wrist is aligned during the technique ensures that both bones and tendons will be damaged, possibly broken.

APPLICATION 15 – DEFENCE AGAINST A FRONT KICK VARIATION

The attacker comes in with a right Front Kick

The defender steps to 4/5 o'clock and performs a left Low Block, continuing to move in an anti-clockwise direction, ending up at roughly 3 o'clock; this should strike just above their knee on the inside of their thigh. This will cause the attacker to 'open up' when they land

The defender then converts the Low Block into an Inner Forearm Back Fist strike to the face whilst shifting into an 'L-Stance'

The defender follows this up with a stepping forward Obverse Punch

SHORT ANALYSIS

As you can see, this technique does not defend against a classic Front Kick, rather it is to be used against what could be termed as a yobbo/soccer kick. A technique such as this starts at either kicking range or indeed the extreme range (as they often require a run-up).

The block does not require much with regard to skill and can hit anywhere along the leg; it will still smother the kick and cause the attacker to land open and off-balance. Due to the nature of the 'yobbo' kick, it is more likely that you will strike into their upper leg, rather than their lower leg, especially if you ensure that you step back and to the side (due to its somewhat circular nature).

Not giving them a chance to recover the Back Fist takes their attention from the Low Section to the High Section and therefore allows the defender to move back in with a stepping punch.

A knee could just as easily be used as part of the step and then followed by a close-in technique such as an Elbow.

I view the earlier technique as a much more valid option however as the maxim of 'leg to leg, arm to arm' should always be borne in mind. That said however, most taekwondo students are taught to Low Block to Front Kicks both in set sparring and in free sparring. As a result of this, the Low Block is most likely to be used as a trained flinch reflex.

It is therefore important that you move diagonally and around rather than straight back in order to lessen the impact on your arm as this will allow you to move inside and along their kick, rather than taking it at its full power.

14

TAEGEUK IL JANG –
HOW TO PERFORM IT

Start in Neutral Stance

Turn 90° left, into left WTF
Walking Stance, Low Block

3

Step forward into right WTF Walking Stance, Obverse Punch

4

Turn 180° right into right WTF Walking Stance, Low Block

5

Step forward into left WTF Walking Stance, Obverse Punch

6

Turn 90° left into left WTF Front Stance, Low Block and immediate right Reverse Punch.

7

Turn 90° right into right WTF Walking Stance (moving right foot), left Inside Block

Step forward into left WTF Walking Stance, right Reverse Punch	Turn 180° left into left WTF Walking Stance, right Inside Block	Step forward into right WTF Walking Stance, left Reverse Punch

Turn 90° right into right WTF Front Stance, Low Block and immediate left Reverse Punch

Turn 90° left (moving left foot) into left WTF Walking Stance, left Rising Block

Right Front Kick, and land into right WTF Walking Stance,
Obverse Punch

Turn 180° right into
right WTF Walking
Stance, Rising Block

Left Front Kick, and land into left WTF Walking Stance,
Obverse Punch

Turn 90° right (moving
left foot) into left WTF
Front Stance, Low Block

Step forward into right
WTF Front Stance, right
Obverse Punch

Turn 180 anti-clockwise
and return to Chunbi

15

TAEGEUK IL JANG – APPLICATIONS

The purpose of this chapter is to demonstrate the applications that can be found within Taegeuk Il Jang. Please bear in mind that these are only pointers. I'm not saying (nor would I ever say) that these are *the* applications, or even the sole applications. Rather, I hope that these applications serve as pointers and help you find your own applications.

As with any percussive martial arts that have a karate base, both ITF and WTF patterns have similar moves. As a result, WTF practitioners can also use the Saju Jirugi applications for moves 1–4 of Taegeuk Il Jang. Please refer to Chapter 13.

APPLICATION I – AGAINST DOUBLE LAPEL GRAB

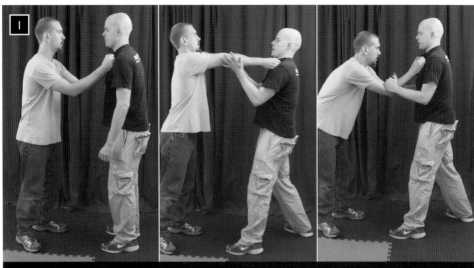

The attacker has grabbed the defender's lapels

Pulling back slightly, the defender brings their palms up into the bottom of the attacker's elbows (or even slightly inwards, bottom for 'zombie' grab application, inwards for street) to distract them. Done with sufficient force, this will raise them onto the balls of their feet

Then coverts the movement into a twin punch into centre mass or groin

The defender then steps off to the right, aiming to turn a full 90° from their original starting position

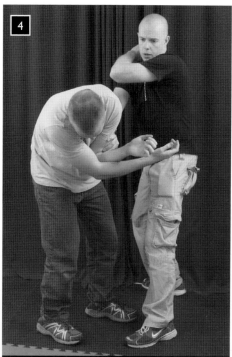

The defender uses their right hand to check the attacker's left arm (same side)

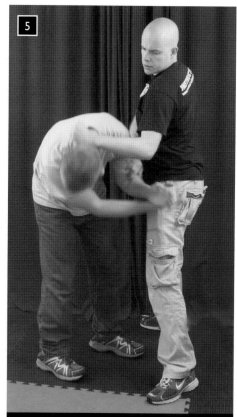

The defender then takes a short step forward with the left leg and left Low Blocks to the side of the attacker's neck or head whilst driving forward into the stance

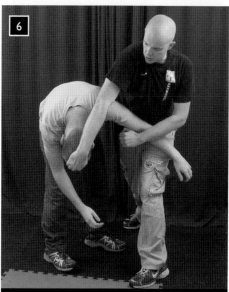

The defender then uses the right punch to grab the attacker's hair at the back of their head

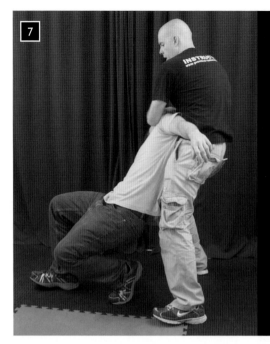

Turning right the defender uses their right hand to pull the attacker's head back and down by the hair whilst using their left hand to assist throwing them. The defender can also kick out with their foot for the Chunbi Sweep to aid in taking them down. Once they are on the floor, the defender finishes as required

SHORT ANALYSIS

It is instinctive for people to pull back when being pulled forward. Therefore the opening of this application corresponds with both the defender's natural instincts and the attacker's natural expectations.

What won't be expected is an attack on the bottom part of the arm, nor the defender's rapid step forward coupled with the twin punch into the centre mass.

The step to the outside allows the defender to close down one of the attacker's weapons whilst giving them a better opportunity to escape should they feel able.

APPLICATION 2 – AGAINST WRIST GRAB

The attacker has grabbed the defender's right wrist with their right hand

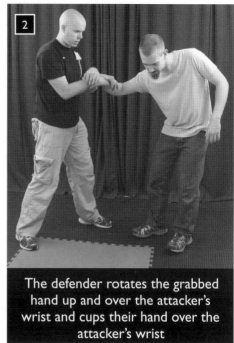

The defender rotates the grabbed hand up and over the attacker's wrist and cups their hand over the attacker's wrist

The defender steps out to 3 o'clock into the long Walking Stance and performs Low Block, pulling the attacker forward and down

The defender performs Reverse Punch to the attacker's head

Reaching past the attacker's head, the
defender places their hand on the
attacker's face

The defender then brings the attacker's head up and back, whilst using
Chunbi Sweep to take them to the ground

During research for the book and the Practical Taekwondo™ system, it was found that this technique does not require strength to be performed. Although using a completely compliant partner, it was found that the technique could be performed exceedingly slowly with the attacker still ending up in the lock and being unable to prevent this through increased grip alone.

However, attackers are not compliant people by nature (hence them being called 'attackers'). This means that the technique should be performed as quickly and sharply as possible in order to both secure the wrist and cause the attacker to step forward.

It is vital that the defender's hands are as close to their body as possible. Imagine a Tyrannosaurus Rex's arms when performing the technique. This keeps the attacker's arm outstretched and increases the pain caused.

The punch to the head is a nice simple technique and the position of the attacker allows the defender to easily sweep them and make their escape.

APPLICATION 3 – PRE-EMPTIVE HAIR GRAB AND THROW

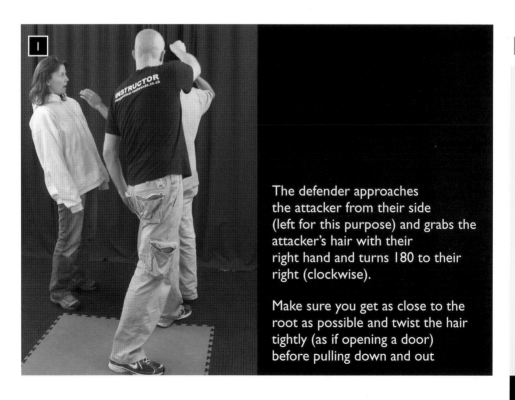

I

The defender approaches the attacker from their side (left for this purpose) and grabs the attacker's hair with their right hand and turns 180 to their right (clockwise).

Make sure you get as close to the root as possible and twist the hair tightly (as if opening a door) before pulling down and out

15

TAEGEUK IL JANG – APPLICATIONS

The defender uses their left hand to assist as they throw the attacker down into 'Low Block'. To do this they cup the attacker's chin

Once the attacker is down on the ground, the defender can finish as necessary

SHORT ANALYSIS

This is a proactive move that completely blindsides the attacker. Whilst they are busy concentrating on the victim in front of them the defender is able to take advantage of the tunnel vision caused by adrenaline and take the attacker by surprise.

Hair pulling, if done properly, can cause immense pain and the eyes to tear up. A sharp yank back and down, coupled with the Palm Heel to the chin will take the attacker off of their feet or cause them to start staggering backwards at the very least. Either way, they are at the mercy of the defender.

APPLICATION 4 – AGAINST RIGHT HAND RIGHT SHOULDER GRAB – TURNING INTO THROW (WITH ATTACKER 90 DEGREES TO YOUR RIGHT)

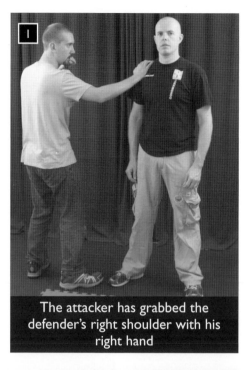

The attacker has grabbed the defender's right shoulder with his right hand

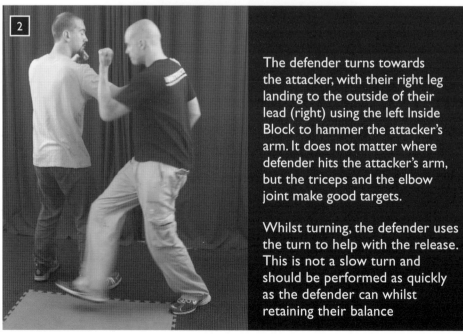

The defender turns towards the attacker, with their right leg landing to the outside of their lead (right) using the left Inside Block to hammer the attacker's arm. It does not matter where defender hits the attacker's arm, but the triceps and the elbow joint make good targets.

Whilst turning, the defender uses the turn to help with the release. This is not a slow turn and should be performed as quickly as the defender can whilst retaining their balance

The defender then steps forward to the outside of the attacker's leg whilst throwing the 'punch' past the attacker's head.

If the defender has to, the defender can now use their knee as an attack and turn into the attacker's knee. This will buckle them and cause them to dip

Although the defender has not struck the attacker with their fist, the defender has taken them off-balance and also severely limited their counter-strike options

The defender then turns to the left (180°) anti-clockwise whilst holding onto the attacker's right shoulder with their left hand

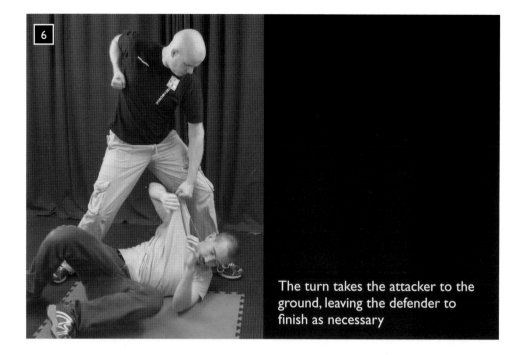

6

The turn takes the attacker to the ground, leaving the defender to finish as necessary

SHORT ANALYSIS

Although there are a lot of steps, this technique is relatively simple with a lot of in-built redundancy with the defender able to use their knees to aid in the defence, along with the missed punch and the reap.

APPLICATION 5 – AGAINST LEFT HAND RIGHT SHOULDER GRAB

The attacker has grabbed the defender's right shoulder with his left hand

The defender turns towards the attacker, with their right leg landing to the outside of the attacker's lead (right) leg

The defender uses the left Inside Block to hammer their arm. It does not matter where defender hits the arm, but the Heart points (see Appendix: Pressure Points), and the inside of the bicep make good targets.

Whilst turning, use the turn to help with the release. This is not a slow turn and should be performed as quickly as the defender can whilst retaining their balance

The defender then punches with their right hand, using this to grab the attacker's head

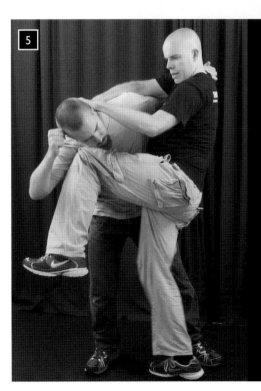

They then use their left leg to knee them. Please note that the level of the knee is totally dependant upon circumstances at the time. If the defender can only get a low-section Knee-Kick in, then they should use that. It is important that the defender never fixates on how a technique 'should' be. Go with the flow and technique be damned

6

The defender lands and turns 180° anti-clockwise and uses their right hand to throw them to the ground again

SHORT ANALYSIS

A cross-hand shoulder grab is often used to make someone turn very quickly as the pull back and across adds to their momentum far more than if the grab was same-side.

This is actually to the defender's advantage, especially if they are aware that such a situation might arise (see following Short Analysis as to why this might be) as it allows them to turn out of the grip whilst using the momentum caused to aid the power of the leg strike.

None of the follow-up techniques require much skill to deliver and all of them are easily used whilst suffering the effects of adrenalin.

APPLICATION 6 – AGAINST LEFT SHOULDER GRAB FROM BEHIND

The attacker grabs the defender's shoulder from behind

The defender uses the right Inside Block to strike the inside of the grabbing arm, striking any of the points located there

The defender then grabs the attacker's head and pulls down

As they pull down they use their right leg to knee. Please note that the level of the knee is totally dependant upon circumstances at the time. If the defender can only get a low-section Knee-Kick in, then they should use that. It is important that the defender never fixate on how a technique 'should' be. Go with the flow and technique-be-damned

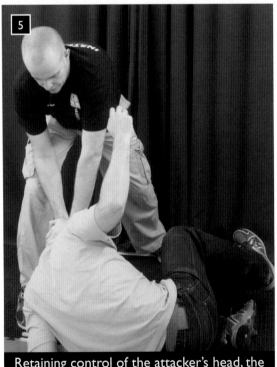

Retaining control of the attacker's head, the defender turns into Low Block throw

SHORT ANALYSIS

During research into this book, the author read through a large number of witness statements regarding assaults. A common theme arose in which the defender was involved in an altercation, turned to leave and was then attacked either through being grabbed as in this technique or punched.

This technique obviously arises from such a situation and should not be used in the event of just anyone grabbing the shoulder. Even friends can be rough sometimes!

By turning the defender is doing four things. First of all they are covering their head in a flinching manner, second they are moving towards the perceived threat and third they are attacking the attacker's legs. Finally they are also winding their body round and giving added momentum to the follow-up knee (should it be required). This is very much a 'go through your attacker' application or as the U.S. Marines would say 'violence of action', that is, you do not stop until the attacker does.

APPLICATION 7 – AGAINST DOUBLE LAPEL GRAB

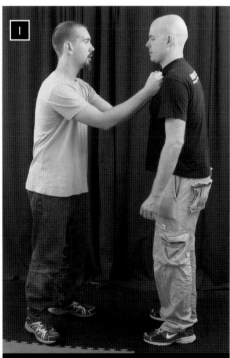

The attacker has grabbed the defender by his shirt

The defender uses left Inside Block into the grabbing arms, whilst forwards and to the outside of the attacker with his right leg

The defender then uses the left hand to grab the hair whilst returning it to the hip. At the same time he punches his right hand forward under the attacker's chin. The attacker's head is now momentarily pinned between the defender's hands

The defender starts to turn to the left. Note how the attacker's right leg is trapped behind the defender's right leg. This prevents him from being able to step out of the application

5

The defender continues to turn to the left, taking the attacker to the ground

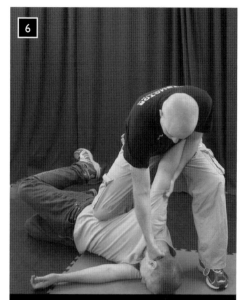

6

Note how the defender is able to land in a dominant position on the attacker, retaining control of both the attacker's head and his right arm

SHORT ANALYSIS

By grabbing the defender with both hands, the attacker has made their aggressive intent obvious. There are three main things that they can do at that moment. They can push or pull the defender, headbutt them or perform a knee attack. The first two are more likely than the latter.

The Inside Block is an instinctive act and is used mainly to set the attacker up for the following techniques. It is useful, however, in that it allows the defender to start regaining the initiative quickly.

The neck twist is a very serious technique to perform, but does not necessarily need to be done at full speed and full power in order to take the attacker to the floor.

If the attacker does not have hair, then it is still possible to gain a firm grip on the back of their head, with the chin being used more as a lever.

APPLICATION 8 – AGAINST RIGHT-HANDED LAPEL GRAB (LEFT LAPEL)

The attacker has grabbed the defender's left lapel, using his right hand

The defender rakes left Inside Block in and down the attacker's arm, trapping the grabbing hand. See Appendix: Pressure Points, for the points that will be struck or rubbed during this

Keeping the grabbing hand trapped the defender punches without moving forward so that the attacker is extended (Palm Heel can also be used)

The defender then uses the left leg forward
movement as a knee attack to GB31
(see Appendix: Pressure Points)

SHORT ANALYSIS

This is a very quick counter-attack and both the trap and strike can and should be performed simultaneously in order to maximise the effect. The rake can bring the attacker forward and down towards the defender quite sharply and when this movement is checked by a solid blow can cause a great deal of penetration for the blow.

The low knee continues the assault and, landing forward, the defender can easily take the attacker to the ground, or continue a more percussive solution.

APPLICATION 9 – AGAINST CROSS-HAND GRAB TO RIGHT HAND FROM FRONT

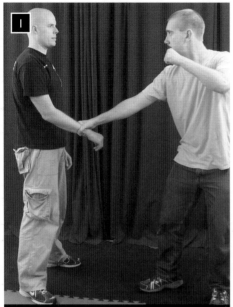

The attacker has grabbed the defender by the right hand with his right hand

The defender brings their left hand under the grabbing hand and lifts sharply upwards, pulling the grabbed hand back to the hip

The defender continues the Rising Block but circles their hand under and over (anti-clockwise) so that the defender can grab the hand

The defender pulls sharply down and uses their weight as a support whilst throwing Front Snap Kick or knee into the legs

The defender lands into stance and punches the attacker in the head

The defender can then take down the attacker or follow up with further strikes

SHORT ANALYSIS

This is basically a Centre Lock in reverse in that it uses the left hand to break the attacker's grip.

Using the left hand allows the defender to move to the inside of the attacker and means that the attacker's stomach, the inside of their knees and thighs and the back of their head are all open to counter-attack.

15

TAEGEUK IL JANG – APPLICATIONS

APPLICATION 10 – AGAINST RIGHT HAYMAKER

The defender is trying to placate the attacker whilst in Defence Stance, making sure that they are keeping their distance

As the attacker goes to strike, the defender steps off to 4 or 5 o'clock with their right leg whilst doing left Rising Block into the inside of the attacking arm, trying to grab and hold

The defender then does right rear Front Kick to the inside of the rear leg or groin

The defender lands and punches or Elbows the attacker

SHORT ANALYSIS

The Rising Block is, when used like this, very similar to the instinctive warding motion that people make whenever an attack comes towards them in such a manner. Therefore it's almost an instinctive rather than trained technique.

Stepping to 4 or 5 o'clock means that the attacking arm has much further to travel, whilst placing the defender on the inside of the attacker. Because of the nature of the attack, the attacker will be left momentarily wide open which in turn allows the defender to move into and through the attacker using the Front Kick to take their balance before following up with further strikes.

It does not matter if the grab fails, what is important is that forward momentum is continued. Bury the kick into the inside of the leg and plant the elbow. It is also important that you should not aim for a specific area on the leg. If you do, you will most likely miss. Just try to kick the leg as a whole.

The attacker has grabbed the defender by their right lapel, using his left hand

The defender traps the grabbing hand with their right hand, steps their left leg forward and twists their right shoulder back, causing the attacker to step forward

The defender then performs Rising Block into the attacker's face or side of neck

The defender then does a right Rear Kick or Knee to the inside of the attacker's thigh

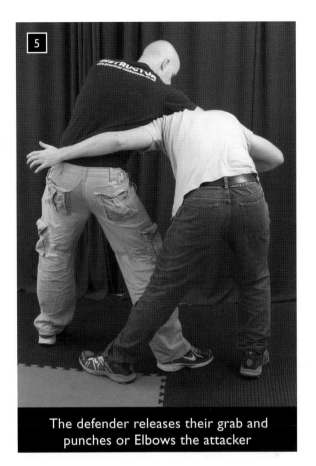

The defender releases their grab and
punches or Elbows the attacker

SHORT ANALYSIS

Short sharp movements are key to disrupting the attacker's balance.
Done slowly they will have time to adjust, done quickly and they will
come forward rapidly and off-balance.

Whilst they are still stepping forwarding the Rising Block to the face or
neck has the opportunity to end the fight there and then. However, the
application has a lot of in-built redundancy which allows the defender to
blitz through the attacker using the knee and hand attacks.

APPLICATION 12 – AGAINST LEFT LAPEL GRAB BY THE RIGHT HAND

The attacker has grabbed the defender with his right hand on the left lapel

The defender performs a left Rising Block into Heart 3 using a Back Fist to strike. See Appendix: Pressure Points

The defender then performs a right rear Front Kick or knee to the attacker's centre mass

Landing forward the defender follows this with a punch or Elbow

15

TAEGEUK IL JANG – APPLICATIONS

SHORT ANALYSIS

This is a very short and to-the-point technique. The fact that the attacker has grabbed the defender is actually in the defender's benefit. No matter whether they have their eyes closed or open, because the attacker has secured a grip on them, the defender will be able to locate the attacker.

This means that striking into the fleshy inside of the attacker's arm is made all the easier. The point struck is located near to the funny bone as well as other points, whatever it hits, it will cause pain. The most optimistic outcome of the strike is that it will effectively 'kill' the arm, whilst causing intense pain. This may also be coupled with the attacker losing their grip, coming up onto their toes, closing their eyes (or wincing) or even blacking out temporarily.

Working on the most pessimistic outcome, however, the strike will still cause sufficient pain to take the attacker's attention away from their attack to the point of pain.

This gives the defender the window of opportunity to perform the knee, and follow it up with any necessary techniques. The initiative is with the defender and it is up to them as to how they finish it.

APPLICATION 13 – AGAINST LEFT LAPEL GRAB BY THE RIGHT HAND

The attacker has grabbed the defender's left lapel using their right hand

2

The defender performs a left Rising Block to the attacker's arm, snaking it under and through so that they can counter-grab them. At the same time they pin the attacking hand to ensure the attacker does not lose their grip.

If you have trouble visualising this, imagine that they are trying to poke the attacker in their throat

3

The defender then uses their right hand to grab the attacker behind the head

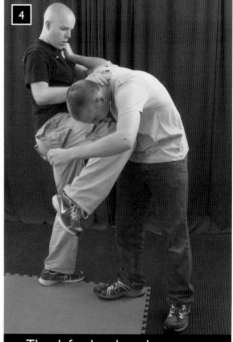

4

The defender then does a rear knee to the inside of the attacker's leg or chest

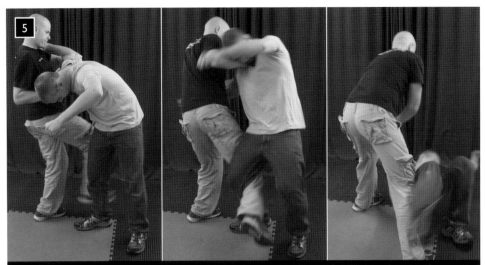

Landing forward, the defender then snakes their leg behind the attacker's, turns to the left and throws the attacker to the floor, ensuring that the attacker is not able to step out of the sweep due to the position of the defender's leg

SHORT ANALYSIS

The mind of the attacker is firmly set on establishing dominance through a number of factors; they have grabbed the defender, it is likely they will be using coarse and threatening language, they may well be pushing forward, backwards or even shaking the defender using the grabbing hand.

The defender can cause a very quick 'shock' to the attacker by reversing this position. The attacker has gifted the defender one of his hands by grabbing, limiting the options for attack to one hand and two legs.

The defender on the other hand has all of their weapons available to them. They are also able to utilise the attacker's body weight to maintain their balance should they need to.

The defender first attacks the top section of the attacker by performing the Rising Block and counter-grab. They then quickly shift the point of attack by kneeing into the sensitive inside thigh.

Finally they combine the two sections by using the hands and legs to complete the sweep.

APPLICATION 14 – AGAINST GRAB TO RIGHT HAND – POSITIONAL INDICATOR TECHNIQUE

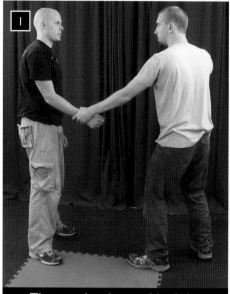

The attacker has grabbed the defender's right hand, using their left hand

The defender turns 90° to their right whilst making sure that the grabbing arm is turned with the elbow downwards

The defender then punches left Rising Block up into the attacker's arm locking it.

Note how the blow will temporarily lift the attacker onto their toes

The defender then rapidly circles his arm back over and around as if they were performing a Lower Outer Forearm Block. This movement finishes with their hand grabbing the front of the attacker's top, or their shoulder

The defender then sweeps the attacker by 'stepping' their left leg forward and pushing their left arm back and down. Note how, in this picture, the attacker's arm is completely locked. An attempt to throw him by myself at this point would have broken the arm, due to the fact it was locked onto my hip.

As an aid to further disorientate the attacker and assist in taking them to the floor, the right hand can be used to grab their hair, snake round on the face/forehead and pull back, or be used for a Chunbi Sweep

SHORT ANALYSIS

Although this technique can be viewed as having lost the initiative due to the attacker securing a grip on the hand, it is not necessarily due to the grip being the initial attack (although it may also be that). The grip may well be due to an action carried out by the defender prior to the grip being applied.

The turn to the right will, if done quickly, cause the attacker to step and momentarily lose their balance. Coupled with the quick strike to the base of the elbow, this will allow the defender to regain the initiative whilst keeping the attacker off-balance right through to the takedown.

Many people will say that a grab to the wrist is not a 'normal' attack. However, I have both grabbed and been grabbed by the wrist whilst working as a door supervisor. It also depends on your sex. Whilst I was a special constable I often witnessed males grabbing women by the wrist and upper arm in an attempt to control them.

Whilst watching fights after closing time, I often see friends grabbing their friends by the wrist and arm in order to prevent them from fighting. Often the other person is not being 'helped' by their friends and is free to launch an attack. Therefore it is important to bear in mind that this sort of grab-based attack does happen, whether it is from friends or enemies is another matter.

APPENDIX: PRESSURE POINTS

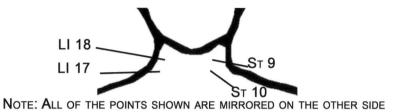

LI 18
LI 17
St 9
St 10

NOTE: ALL OF THE POINTS SHOWN ARE MIRRORED ON THE OTHER SIDE

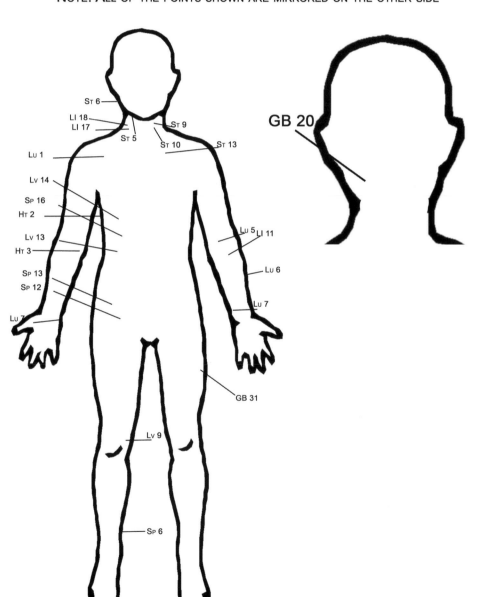

St 6
LI 18
LI 17
St 5
St 9
St 10
St 13
Lu 1
Lv 14
Sp 16
Ht 2
Lv 13
Ht 3
Sp 13
Sp 12
Lu 7
Lu 5
LI 11
Lu 6
Lu 7
GB 31
Lv 9
Sp 6

GB 20

BIBLIOGRAPHY

Burgar, Bill *Five Years One Kata* (2003, Martial Arts Publishing)

Clark, Rick *Martial Arts for the University* (1993, Kendall Hunt Pub Co)

Clark, Rick *Pressure-Point Fighting: A Guide to the Secret Heart of Asian Martial Arts* (2000, Tuttle Publishing)

Clark, Rick *75 Down Blocks: Refining Karate Technique* (2003, Tuttle Publishing)

Hee Park, Yeon et al. *Tae Kwon Do* (1999, Facts on File Inc.)

Il Cho, Hee *The Complete Tae Kwon Do Kyung* (1984, Unique Publications)

Rhee, Jhoon *Chon-Ji of Tae Kwon Do Hyung* (1970, Black Belt Communications)

Tedeschi, Marc *Taekwondo: Traditions, Philosophy Technique* (2003, Weatherhill Inc)

Wagner, Jim *Reality-Based Personal Protection* (2005, Black Belt Books)

KOREAN A-Z

A

Ah-gumson – Choking Hand (WTF)

Ahop – Nine

An Palmok – Inner Forearm

An Palmok Makgi – Inner Forearm Block

Anaero – Inward

Anaero Bandal Chagi – Inward Crescent Kick

Annun Sogi – Sitting Stance

Ap Cha Milgi – Front Pushing Kick

Ap Chabusigi – Front Snap Kick

Ap Chaolligi – Front Rising Kick

Ap Joomuk – Fore Fist

Ap Kumchi – Ball of foot

Apro Kaggi – Forward

B

Bae Sim – Juror (WTF)

Baekjool Boolgool – Indomitable Spirit

Bakaero – Outward

Bakaero Bandal Chagi – Outward Crescent Kick

Bakat Palmok Outer Forearms

Bakat Palmok Makgi – Outer Forearm Block

Baldal Dung – Reverse Footsword

Baldung – Instep

Balkal – Footsword

Ban Jayoo Matsoki – Semi-free sparring

Bandae Dollyo Chagi – Reverse Turning Kick/
  Spinning Roundhouse Kick

Bandae Dollyo Golcho Chagi – Reverse
  Hooking Kick (Spinning Hooking Kick)

Bandae Jirugi – Reverse Punch

Bandal Chagi – Crescent Kick

Bandal Jirugi – Crescent Punch

Bandal San – Arc Hand

Ba-quo – Switch (WTF)

Baro Jirugi – Obverse Punch

Barrol – Return to Ready Stance

Biture Chagi – Twisting Kick

Bu Sim – Judge (WTF)

Bubun – Section

Bungai – Application

C

Cha Bapgi – Stamping Kick

Chagi – Kick (NOTE: the cha and gi may often
  be split, for example, CHAolliGI)

Chapki – Grappling Techniques

Charyot – Attention

Charyot Sogi – Attention Stance

Chi-gi – Strike (WTF)

Chil – Seventh

Chil Sik Sul – Choking Techniques

Chon-ji Tul – Pattern Chon-Ji 19 Moves Lit:

Heaven and Earth. The pattern consists of two similar parts, one for heaven and one for Earth.

Chookyo Makgi – Rising Block

Choong-Moo Tul – Pattern Chung-Moo 30 Moves Lit: The given name of the great Admiral Yi Sun-Sin of the Yi Dynasty. He was reputed to have invented the first armoured battleship (Kobukson) which was the precursor of the present day submarine in 1592 AD. The reason why this pattern ends up with a left hand attack is to symbolise his regrettable death having had no chance to show his potential due to his loyalty to his King.

Chunbi – Ready

D

Dagger – Tando

Dan – Rank for black belt holders

Dan Gun Tul – Pattern Dan Gun 21 Moves Lit: Is named after the Holy Dan Gun, legendary founder of Korea in the year 2333 BC.

Dari – Leg

Dasaul – Five

Digutja Makgi – U-shaped Block

Do San Tul -– Pattern Do San 24 Moves Lit: The pseudonym of the patriot Ahn Chang-Ho (1876–1938). The 24 moves represent his life, which he dedicated to furthering the education of Korea and its independence movement.

Dobok – Training Suit

Dojang – Training Hall

Dollymio Makgi – Circular Block

Dollyo Chagi – Turning Kick

Dollyo Jirugi – Turning Punch

Dollyon Joo – Forging Post

Donzigi – (WTF)

Doo Bandalson Makgi – Double Archand Block

Doo Palmok Makgi – Double Forearm Block

Doro Chagi – Waving Kick

Dul – Two

Dung Joomuk – Back Fist

Dung Joomuk Taerigi – Back Fist Strike

Dunjigi wa torojigi – Throwing Techniques

Duro Gamyo Chagi – Skip Kick

Duro Makgi – Scooping Block

Dwijibin Sonkut – Upset Fingertip

Dwijibo Jirugi – Upset Punch

Dwit – Back

Dwit Bal Sogi – Rear Foot Stance

Dwit Chagi – Back Kick

Dwit Chook – Back Heel

Dwit Kumchi – Back Sole

Dwiyro Kaggi – Backwards

Dwiyro Torro – About Turn

E

E – Second

El – First

Eolgul – Face

G

Gam Ju m – Deduction of Point (WTF)

Gamsa Hamnida – Thank you (WTF)

Ghin Joomuk – Long Fist

Gojong Sogi – Fixed stance

Golcho Chagi – Hooking Kick

Golcho Makgi – Hooking Block

Goman – Stop

Gomson – Bear Hand

Gong-kyok – Offence

Googup Hwal Bop – Healing through the use of acupressure (WTF)

Goorugi – Rolling/tumbling

Goro Chagi – Sweeping Kick

Guburyo Sogi – Bending Stance

Guk Gee – Self-control

Guk-gi – Flag (WTF)

Gunnun Sogi – Walking Stance

Gup/Kup – Rank for coloured belt holders

H

Habansin – Foot parts

Haessan – Dismiss

Hanna – One

Hechyo – Spreading (WTF)

Hechyo Makgi – Wedging Block

Him – Energy (internal energy or lifeforce) (WTF)

Ho Shin Sul – Self-defence applications

Homi Sonkut – Angle Fingertip

Honap Chagi – Combination Kicks

Hori Makgi – Waist Block

Hullyo Makgi – Sweeping Blocks

Huri – Waist

Hwa Rang Tul – Pattern Hwa Rang 29 Moves Lit: Flowering Youth. Named after the Hwa Rang Youth Group which originated in the Silla Dynasty about 600 AD. This group eventually became the actual driving force for the unification of the three Kingdoms of Korea. The 29 movements refer to the 29th Infantry Division where taekwondo developed into maturity. Hyel Do Sul – Vital Point Techniques.

Hyung – Pattern

I

Ibo Matsoki – Two step sparring

Ilbo Matsoki – One step sparring

Ilgop – Seven

In Nae – Perseverance

Inji Chigwon – Foreknuckle Fist

Integrity – Yom Chi

Ip – Mouth

J

Jappyosul Tae – Release from grab

Jayoo Matsoki – Free sparring

Jeja –Student

Jeon – Round (competition segment) (WTF)

Jeum – Point (competition) (WTF)

Jipge son – Finger Pincers

Jirugi – Punch

Jongsin Tongil – Meditation (WTF)

Joo Sim – Referee (WTF)

Joong Gun Tul – Pattern Joong Gun 30 Moves Lit: Named after the patriot An Joong Gun who assassinated Hiro Bumi Ito, the Japanese Governor General of Korea, known as the man who played the leading part of the Korea-Japan merger. There are 32 movements in this pattern to represent Mr An's age when he was executed in the Lui-Shung prison in 1910.

Jupgi – Hold/Holding (WTF)

K

Ka Soom Ho Goo – Chest Protector (WTF)

Kae Sim – Time keeper (WTF)

Kae Sok – Continue (WTF)

Kalyeu – Break/Stop (WTF)

Kaunde – Middle

Ki Rohk – Recorder (WTF)

Kihop/Kihap – Yell (to collect and focus internal energy)

Koo – Ninth

Kwan – School (a place where TKD is taught) (WTF)

Kwan Jyel Sul – Joint Manipulation Technique

Ki Bon Sul – Basic Techniques

Kwanjangnim – Master Instructor (above fifth degree black belt) (WTF)

Kyocha Makgi – X-Block

Kyocha Sogi – X-stance

Kyong-ye – Bow

Kyorugi – Sparring (WTF)

M

Ma-ai – Distance

Ma Hyel – Pressure point which induces paralysis

Me-joomuk chi-gi – Hammer Fist Strike

Miro Makgi – Pushing Block

Moa Sogi – Closed Stance

Modoo – Gathering

Mok – Neck

Mo-li – Head

Mom Chagi – Checking Kick

Momchau Makgi – Checking Block

Momtong Bachia – Press Ups

Momtong – Body

N

Nachuo Sogi – Low Stance

Naeryo Chagi – Downward Kick

Naeryo Makgi – Downward Block

Najunde – Low

Najunde Chagi – Low Kick

Nak Sul – Falling Techniques

Narani Sogi – Parallel Stance

Net – Four

Niunja Sogij – 'L' Stance

Noollo Chagi – Pressing Kick

Noollo Makgi – Pressing Block

Nopunde – High

Nopunde Chagi – High Kick

O

O – Fifth

Ollyo Jirugi – Upward punch

Opun Sonkut Tulgi – Flat Fingertip Thrust

Orun – Right

P

Palkup – Elbow

Palmok – Forearm

Palmok Daebi Makgi – Forearm Guarding
Block

Pang'on – Defence Techniques

Pang Wi (also Pang Wee) – Defence Against

Pi Hagi – Dodging

Pul – Eighth

Pyon Joomuk – Knuckle Fist (WTF)

Pyon Joomuk Chi-gi – Knuckle Fist Strike
(WTF)

Pyung Joomuk – Open Fist

S

Sa – Fourth

Sabomnim – Instructor (above fourth degree
black belt) (WTF)

Sabum – Instructor

Saju Jirugi – Four-Directional Punch (Beginner's
punch block exercise)

Sam – Third

Sambo Matsoki – Three Step sparring

San Makgi – W Shape Block

Sang Bal Chagi – Twin Foot Kick

Sang Dwijibo Jirugi – Twin Upset Punch

Sang Ii – Jacket

Sang Joomuk – Twin Fist

Sang Palkup – Twin Elbow

Sang Palmok Makgi – Twin Forearm Block

Sang Sonkal – Twin knife hand

Sangbasin – Hand Parts

Set – Three

Sewo Chagi – Vertical Kick

Sewo Jirugi – Vertical Punch

Shi Gan – Time (time out) (WTF)

Shim Gong Sul – Mind Training Techniques

Shim Ho Hyup – Breathing Control (WTF)

Sib – Tenth

Si-jak – Start

Sin-Chong (also "Sin-Ch'ong) – Application

Sul Sin-Chong – Technique Application

Sa Hyel – Lethal pressure points

Son – Straight

Son badak – Palm Strike

Son Dung – Backhand (WTF)

Son Garrak – Two Finger

Son Sonkut Tulgi – Straight Spear Finger thrust

Sonbadak – Palm

Sonkal – Knifehand

Sonkal Daebi Makgi – Knifehand Guarding Block

Sonkal Dung – Ridge Hand

Sonkal Taerigi – Knifehand Strike

Sonkut – Fingertips

Sonmock – Wrist

Sonmuk Dong – Bent/Bow wrist

Soojik Sogi – Vertical Stance

Soopyong – Horizontal

Sun Sonkut – Spear finger

T

Tae – Hand

Ti – Belt

Toi Gye Tul – Pattern Toi Gye 37 Moves Lit: The pen name of the noted scholar Yi Hwang (16 C AD) an authority on neo-confucianism. The 37 movements of the pattern refer to his birthplace on the 37° latitude; the diagram represents the scholar.

Too Sul – Throwing Techniques

Tong Hyel – Pressure point which induces pain

Tul – Patterns

Tulgi – Thrust

Twigi – Jumping

Twigi Ap Chagi – Jumping Front Kick

Twigi Yop Chagi – Jumping Side Kick

Twimyo – Flying

Twimyo Bandal Chagi – Flying Crescent Kick

Twimyo Chagi – Flying Kick

Twimyo Nopi Chagi – Flying High Kick

Twimyo Yop Chagi – Flying Side Kick

Twio Nomo Chagi – Overhead Kick

U

Umji Changwon – Thumb Knuckle Fist

W

Wae Bal Sogi – One leg stance

Wen – Left

Wi Palkup Taerigi – Upward Elbow Strike

Won Hyo Tul – Pattern Won Hyo 28 Moves Lit: The noted monk who introduced Buddhism in the Silla dynasty in the year 686 AD.

Y

Yasaul – Six

Ye wi – Courtesy

Yodoll – Eight

Yoll – Ten

Yonsok Chagi – Consecutive Kick

Yop Bal Badak – Side Sole

Yop Cha Tulgi – Side Thrust Kick

Yop Chajirugi – Side Piercing Kick Lit: Side Punch Kick

Yop Chaolligi – Side Rising Kick

Yop Jirugi – Side punch

Yop Joomuk – Side Fist

Yugwon – Hammer Fist

Yuk – Sixth

Yul Gok Tul – Pattern Yul Gok 38 Moves Lit: The pseudonym of a great philosopher and scholar Yi (1536–1584 AD) nicknamed the Confucious of Korea. The 38 movements refer to his birthplace on the 38° latitude and the diagram represents the scholar.